GENERATION
SCREWED

CANDICE MALCOLM

To my parents.

I don't hold you personally responsible.

CONTENTS

TIP: MILLIONS VS. BILLIONS

Most people are not used to hearing and thinking about the large numbers we encounter in government budgeting. It's difficult to imagine what a million dollars looks like, let alone the billions and trillions we have accumulated in government debt. To help keep in mind the difference between a million dollars and a billion dollars, remember this simple bar trick:

If I gave you a dollar per second, how long would it take for me to give you a million dollars?

Answer: About 12 days.

And if I gave you a dollar per second, how long would it take for me to give you a billion dollars?

Answer: About 32 years.

And as for a trillion dollars? Well, at a rate of a dollar per second, it would take longer than some the earliest records of human history, or over 3,000 years.

DEAR GENERATION SCREWED

"Today is already the tomorrow which the bad economist of yesterday urged us to ignore."

— Henry Hazlitt, *Economics in One Lesson,* 1946

"From each as they choose, to each as they choose."

— Robert Nozick, *Anarchy, State and Utopia*, 1974

Dear Generation Screwed,

It was my sincere pleasure to speak on your campus last month. It's incredible to witness such interest for liberty-oriented student groups like *Generation Screwed* and *Students for Liberty* at a Canadian university. We've come a long way. When I was an undergraduate at the University of Alberta — less than a decade ago — there was no such thing as campus libertarians, aside from perhaps a few student activists within the Marijuana Party.

You asked how and when I became a libertarian, given we didn't have liberty-minded student groups, Sun News Network or figures like Ron Paul and John Stossel. (Well, Stossel was around, he just wasn't asking the right questions about big government back then.) Like most libertarians, for as long as I can remember, I've opposed the status quo and challenged authority. For as long as I've been politically aware (I was a late bloomer, not really caring about politics until after high school), I've opposed central power and the federal government. Growing up in Vancouver, it didn't make a lot of sense to me that decisions affecting my life were made thousands of kilometres away by strangers and people who felt like foreigners in Ottawa. I felt little to no connection with central Canada, Quebec or the Maritimes, aside from hating the Leafs and the Habs. I had a growing acrimony towards Canada's government; the more I learned about the structure and its schemes, from Equalization to EI to the Senate, the more I resented that BC conceded so much power to the control-freaks in the federal government.

My political persuasion evolved during university, and I came to my political views the painful way; that is, through reading, thinking, debating, and spending a bit too much time in university pubs, having pints and discussing politics.

I went through many stages in my thinking, and spent a lot of time reading and defining my worldview. I was interested in many philosophers, from Karl Marx to Adam Smith, and from Plato and Aristotle to John Locke and John Stewart Mill. But none caught my attention or stirred excitement quite like the works of Robert Nozick, the contemporary moral philosopher — who my professor described as "a crackpot and widely discredited thinker who probably read a bit too much Ayn Rand." I didn't care. I pored through the pages of *Anarchy, State & Utopia* and became convinced that the government must be restricted to the narrowest functions. I could imagine a post-government society where all interactions were voluntary and people were not treated as means to an end of some Welfare State or New

Deal society. As Immanuel Kant described in his theory of morality, people are ends in and of themselves. We are not means to some other end. As such, individual liberty is the primary goal of a free society.

It was invigorating, however frivolous, particularly since there was nobody else at my school (at least of the people I knew) who shared my views or my affinity for liberty. This is part of the fun of being a campus libertarian. While you occasionally agree with liberals and socialists on first principles and moral issues, and you often agree with conservatives on fiscal and economic matters, you most often disagree with everyone and can therefore spend much time debating everybody (including know-it-all professors) with thought experiments and hypotheticals, and honing your arguments in the process. Libertarians, classical liberals and free market conservatives should easily be the most well-read and well-prepared graduates of a political science or economics department. We have few allies on campus and plenty of adversaries. This is a blessing. It prepares you for a future as a public intellectual and freedom champion.

From the enlightenment thinkers and Robert Nozick, I went on to read the works of Milton Friedman, Friedrich Hayek and more contemporary writers such as Thomas Sowell, William Easterly and Hernando de Soto. I became even more convinced that a voluntary and free society was far more moral and far more effective at helping people than the centrally planned one. I'm still more convinced than ever that our worldview is the correct one, and that is why it is gratifying and exciting to see so many passionate young libertarian students in my own backyard.

And to answer your question, yes, I've enclosed a copy of my suggested reading list for those who wish to understand the first principles and read the many convincing arguments for liberty and free markets. Please circulate it to any interested friends and classmates. Heck, even ask your professors to have a read.

I've started out on a rather optimistic note, but sadly, the tone of the rest of what I have to say is far more tainted with skepticism, deep criticism and flat-out fearfulness about what lies ahead. The topic of this book, much like my talk at your school, focuses on the ensuing financial crisis that will come from our fiscally unsound big government. The reason this is *your* problem and why you are *generation screwed* is because the largest generation of Canadians is beginning to retire and leave the work force. Once they retire, so too will a big portion of the taxes they contribute into the government's coffers. And thanks to all those big promises made to seniors by politicians, their government entitlements are on a trajectory to bankrupt our government.

The crux of the welfare state — our modern system of government redistribution that makes everyone, not just the poor or the downtrodden but *everyone*, reliant on government — is mortally flawed. It is based on the assumption of permanent and never-ending growth and forever kicking the can down the road to future taxpayers.

The problem for *generation screwed* is that you will be forced to pay into this system, but looking at the math, there is very little chance these programs will still exist by the time you retire. You will be limited in your ability to save for yourself because you will be forced by the government to pay into its schemes and pay for other people's retirement. How can you put aside enough for yourself when your taxes and contribution rates are constantly hiked? You cannot. You do not have a choice about where your money goes. The government has taken the choice away from you.

The concept for this book is not new. For decades, we've heard critics malign the system under which young people inherit the failed policies and public debt accumulated by previous generations. We have heard warnings that our social welfare programs are not properly funded, that big promises made by politicians are not affordable and that these financial shortfalls will proliferate when baby boomers retire. The Canadian Taxpayers Federation adopted the phrase "Generation Screwed" as a campus initiative to wake up young people to the gaping financial problems they will face. The realities of unrealistic spending promises made first *to* baby boomers and then *by* baby boomers.

Paying for the promises of yesterday, being delivered today, with massive bills tomorrow.

Much of today's public policy debates revolve around using borrowed cash and handing off debt to future taxpayers; taxpayers who are drafted to foot the bill for our pay-as-you-go pensions, health care, social assistance, the bloated bureaucracy and every other social handout being dreamt up by civil servants, politicians and political aides.

I have now had the opportunity to present the thesis of this book on university campuses across Canada. In the more recent presentations, I developed a metaphor for *generation screwed*: we are on the Titanic and heading towards a massive iceberg. The tip of the iceberg — the problems that can be seen — are the annual deficits, the accumulated debt and the taxes we pay now to cover the cost (or most of the cost) of our spending addictions and our massive, ever-expanding government.

The rest of the iceberg lies below the surface of the water. Canada's social welfare programs — pensions, health care, elderly benefits and the administrative costs of government — have all not been properly funded. As the spending trajectories soar, young people will face continual premium hikes to keep these programs from bankruptcy, although it is unlikely they will survive. These problems are rarely discussed, although most recognize they are a ticking time bomb for our public finances.

Beyond sustainable funding, this book makes the argument that it is morally wrong to draft young people and future taxpayers, without consent and against their will, to pay for big government programs that may well be bankrupt by the time those future taxpayers could ever enjoy the benefits.

I won't try to hide the fact that I myself am of the libertarian persuasion; my message, therefore, is infused by deep skepticism towards the government and its ability to fix the problems that the government itself created. This book, however, is not merely meant for a libertarian audience. We are all screwed if we do not act soon to fix the fiscal imbalance, address the structural deficits and strike a new arrangement that is more equitable, affordable and structurally sound for everyone. Everyone in this generation is screwed — not just libertarians who are ringing the alarm bell — because everyone will be forced to pay for the benefits of others that they themselves will not receive.

When the system runs out of cash, that's it. Game over. No one gets anything. Even those "entitled to their entitlements" cannot cash the cheques of a government in receivership. Just look at what happened in Detroit. Or Sacramento. Or Greece. Margaret Thatcher famously said, "the problem with socialism is eventually you run out of other people's money." That, in a nutshell, is *generation screwed*. What this book says is: the problem with the welfare state is eventually you run out of other people's money. And that "eventually" is now, as the baby boomers retire. The whole house of cards is about to come tumbling down.

The crux of this argument is not ideology. This is an argument based on math. The numbers just don't add up. And things are only going to get worse.

By exposing the fallible structure of government spending schemes and calling out the politicians on their deception, *generation screwed* can turn things around. We can hold politicians accountable for the costs of their promises, demand a better deal and cut off the system of big government from its lifeline. It must be done to ensure that this generation does not hand the same fate and fiscal burden to our children and grandchildren, as what we ourselves inherited.

This generation is *generation screwed.*

The fight for liberty is certainly an uphill battle. But we have much to be optimistic about, aside from simply knowing that our ideas are right. Aside from telling you the truth about public finances, this book also offers a roadmap on how to change course. How to break down the walls of our debt-induced spending addictions and build a better country for everyone. In order to do this, we will need to expose the truth and change the climate of ideas here in Canada. This will require the challenging task of convincing people that liberty is better than dependency. In the meantime, this book also provides real policy solutions and reforms on the road to building an equitable and fair, post-welfare state Canada.

This transformation is inevitable. Simply put, the government has overextended itself. It cannot afford all the very expensive promises it has made over time to so many citizens. But the transformation presents a tremendous opportunity to re-establish the core tenants of liberty and a free society in Canada.

I very much look forward to seeing what *generation screwed* presents.

In liberty,

Candice

PART I

THE PROBLEM

"The problem with socialism is eventually you run out of other people's money."

— Margaret Thatcher, interview with *Thames TV*, 1976

"The curious task of economics is to demonstrate to men how little they really know about what they imagine they can design."

— Friedrich Hayek, *The Fatal Conceit*, 1990

Our system of government is flawed. Democracy is a brokerage of competing interests and visions, in which special interest groups and coalitions have risen to comprise the bulk of political power; they therefore control decision-making and government policy. These competing interests are often put ahead of everyday citizens and taxpayers. And even when taxpayers and citizens have a say, it is only rational for them to vote for whichever party or politician will give them the biggest package of goods and the lowest possible cost. As jazz icon Albert King sang, "everybody wants to go to heaven, but nobody wants to die." Everyone wants free government services, but nobody wants to pay the price tag.

Our market is equally flawed. It is a "mixed economy" or welfare state that consists of compromises between socialism (a planned economy) and capitalism (a free economy). Despite Canada's high ranking on the Economic Freedom of the World Index, our economy is far from free. Every economic activity imaginable is governed by heavy-handed regulations and met with multiple taxes, levied throughout the supply chain. Scores of government bureaucrats from all three levels of government constantly scour the economy looking for new "revenue tools" and opportunities to tax citizens. Incentives matter in public policy, and many of these rules prevent folks from starting or expanding business ventures. Canada has a serious lack of entrepreneurs. We are a risk-averse country, where corporate Canada and the government enjoy a cushy friendship of mutual rewards. Small competitors and disrupters are few and far between.

The welfare state mixed-economy system was designed to help the poor and needy, but it has been expanded to give free stuff to everyone. Government interference in the market has led to a new form of crony capitalism that rewards the establishment and provides benefits for the well-connected. Our system of government redistribution similarly benefits the first in queue, not necessarily those most in need.

In Ottawa and provincial capitals, it's connections that count. Those who have the best lobbyists and with ties to a government are the ones who tend to win government contracts and receive "grants", "partnerships" and access to "innovation funds."

The Stephen Harper government tried to stem the flood of political aides-turned-lobbyists that plague our political process, by passing the *Accountability Act* in 2006. Among other features, this law prevents political staff from lobbying for five years after working in government. This law does not, however, extend to provincial governments, where this transition is still easy and encouraged. Lobbying firms poach political aides who will give them inside information and help navigate the system of government handouts and special deals as only an insider can.

This political interference in the marketplace undermines the democratic process and gives us a watered-down version of capitalism, filled with cronies and cheaters trying to get special privileges. It only faintly resembles a free market. The problem for *generation screwed* is that both our political and economic systems have been corrupted, and *generation screwed* will have to pay for a reward system that benefits some at the expense of most.

Got Milk?

The special interest lobbies don't just fight for handouts and subsidies; they also encourage laws and regulations to prevent competition. If you are part of a powerful lobby — say, a dairy farmer — the government will protect you from competition and enable you to make more money.

In the case of dairy farmers, federal laws limit the number of permits (known as quotas) distributed for dairy cows in Canada. This practice artificially caps the supply of dairy entering the Canadian market, thereby allowing dairy farmers to charge a higher price for their products. By limiting the competition for milk farmers, and creating this distorting protection to folks within the dairy business, Canadians are forced to pay higher prices for dairy products such as milk and cheese. Canada's dairy industry is easily one of the most complicated and convoluted "markets" in the country.

There are layers of bureaucracy standing between you and your favourite type of cheese at the grocer. Several government agencies, from the Canadian Dairy Commission to provincial dairy marketing boards, control the supply each farmer may produce and set the price consumers must pay. Along with this supply management of dairy, these laws also heavily restrict dairy imports by imposing tariffs on incoming dairy. This makes foreign products even more expensive than our domestically produced and protected ones.

This special interest pandering means that Canadians pay significantly more than our American neighbours for dairy products. A 2014 study by the Conference Board of Canada found that the average Canadian family pays about $276 more for dairy products each year thanks to this policy. In some provinces, particularly western provinces, the cost of acquiring a quota can be pricey. Initially these quotas were free; they now, however, range from $20,000 to $30,00 per dairy cow. The typical dairy farmer in Canada has 70 cows, meaning your average dairy farmer owns about $2.1 million in government-protected quotas. You can see how it would be nearly impossible for new farmers and more competition to enter the market.

How is this egregious, distorting practice permitted? Especially in an industry considered so essential to the health and development of young and growing Canadian children (go into any grocery store and see how many unhealthy drinks are significantly cheaper than milk). Why don't Canadians demand more fairness? Why don't politicians stand up for the consumer? Because of what economists call "concentrated benefits" and "diffuse costs". Dairy farmers, who benefit from the quota system, really benefit. Most dairy farmers in Canada are literally millionaires. It pays dividends to hold on to this monopolistic advantage, and so they do.

Through high-priced lobbyists, they ensure no politician is brave enough to put an end to this lucrative advantage. We call this behaviour rent-seeking. These folks hire fancy lobbyists to pressure politicians and bureaucrats and score special economic advantages. Rent-seekers benefit greatly from government schemes and protection, and these benefits are concentrated to a small number of people. The diffuse costs, on the other hand, are spread out across so many people that it's in nobody's personal interest to lobby against the subsidy or an obscure government program. Are you going to pay for an expensive lobbyist, year in and year out, to potentially save $1.00 every time you buy a carton of milk? Probably not. But you can sure bet that the dairy farmer is willing to pay handsomely to keep the subsidies that made him a millionaire.

Theft, by any other name

It doesn't always take lobbyists to create this imbalance in Canadian public policy. Sometimes, politicians represent themselves and push ideas that benefit politicians over the public. Take the example of the decision to cancel the building of two gas plants prior to and during the Ontario provincial election in 2011. In the midst of an election that saw the incumbent Liberals and challenging PCs neck and neck in the polls, the Liberal war room made a political decision to cancel the unpopular gas plant in Mississauga, despite it already being half constructed, and another in Oakville.

The Liberals benefited enormously from this decision, since mounting NIMBY ("Not In My Back Yard") activism threatened their stronghold in the vote-rich suburbs of Toronto. The announcement to cancel the gas plants contributed to the Liberals winning several local seats and holding on to a slim minority government. The auditor general was later tasked with finding the actual costs of this admittedly political decision, which the Liberals promised would be no higher than $40 million. After an in-depth audit, we learned the total cost for the two cancelled plants was upwards of a jaw-dropping $1.1 billion.

Folks who were paying attention were outraged. But the general public? They may have heard of a "gas plant scandal" — but they likely never learned all the sordid details. They don't really pay attention and they don't really care. In fact, it makes absolutely no difference in their lives. Or at least, no noticeable difference. Why? Because, as we learned from the auditor general, the bulk of the costs for the un-built plants would be borne by all Ontario electricity customers over the next ten years.

According to the 2011 census, there are about five million households in Ontario. The cost for these cancelled plants will be shared between industrial and household ratepayers, so assume that half of the $1.1 billion will be charged to household hydro customers across the province. That breaks down to $112.50 per household, or $11.25 per year over ten years. Since most people pay their hydro bills monthly, they can expect to pay an additional 94 cents per month. Outrageous? Not really. The truth of the matter is, no one is ever going to notice an additional 94 cents per month on their electricity bill. No one will protest on the street or occupy Queen's Park. This is the reality of concentrated benefits and diffuse costs. This is why the Ontario Liberals got away with such a cunning and disgraceful crime.

Our political and economic systems are deeply flawed. These two sad examples are just a sneak peak into the world of favouritism and protection that exists within Canadian governments. This is a major problem for *generation screwed*. As you become politically aware, you will quickly learn that things are stacked heavily against you. And as the rent-seekers seek rent, the taxpayers pay tax. You the consumer and you the ratepayer not only pay the price for bad government policies, regulations and protections that artificially raise the price of everything, but also, you the taxpayer will get slapped with more taxes on top of high prices. The typical Canadian taxpayer pays about 45 cents of every dollar earned to government, as special interests get rich.

And things are about to get worse, because our government is about to get a lot more expensive. And that is part of the central problem for *generation screwed*.

So, what is generation screwed?

You may be wondering, what exactly is *generation screwed?* It is my generation. I was born in the 1980s, or what demographers consider the "Millennial" generation. Millennials are typically considered those born between the early 1980s to the early 2000s. Yes, we are the first generation to enter into adulthood in the 21st century, but I believe *generation screwed* is a more apt and descriptive title for our generation. We are screwed. We will be forced to prop up a system of government that doesn't pay its bills and is therefore headed full steam towards bankruptcy. By the time *generation screwed* reaches the age of typical retirement, there will very likely no longer have a social safety net; its programs will have long gone bankrupt. No government health care. No social welfare. No pensions. Despite paying into these programs throughout our entire working lives, these funds will not be there for us.

Generation screwed is the generation of young Canadians — both those typically considered Generation X and Millennials — that will inherit the largest public debt load in our history. Paying off massive sums of public debt and fixing the public finances will be a daunting task. It will define this generation of young Canadians. That is why we are *generation screwed.*

A 20-year-old Canadian reading this book in 2015 is personally responsible for $17,553 in federal debt, another $17,832 in provincial debt on average, and approximately $82,563 in unfunded liabilities (government promises made but not yet paid for or properly funded, like health care and pensions). Each and every Canadian is on the hook for $117,948 in total government debt and liabilities. If you break it down even further to account for the fact that not every Canadian contributes taxes to the government, the total debt burden rises to $243,476 per taxpayer in Canada. And when that 20-year-old Canadian eventually gets married and maybe has two children? Their total family debt responsibility will become approximately $471,792, and counting.[1]

This institutional debt burden comes from decades of neglect by politicians, and a system that rewards short-term decision making over long-term prosperity. Young Canadians have no choice but to inherit this colossal government debt and our country's convoluted finances. Soon, *generation screwed* will begin to carry out the balancing act. They will be asked to kick the can down the road to their children, just as their parents have done for them.

Just as likely a scenario, however, is that many of these indebted schemes will collapse. And when they do, Canadians will face the

---

[1] Figures from the Fraser Institute's Canadian Government Debt 2014: A guide to the Indebtedness of Canada and the Provinces, April 2014

cold reality behind the friendly facade of big government and the welfare state.

The key features of *generation screwed* are caused by three driving forces, the "3 D's:" Dependency, Demographics and Debt.

Dependency:

After years of being forced to contribute to government entitlement schemes through high taxes, young Canadians will consequently neglect their own personal savings funds like Registered Retirement Savings Plan (RRSP) or Tax Free Savings Account (TFSA). This government dependency, alongside stagnant wages and record household debt, will mean this generation — *generation screwed* — will be poorer than their parents and grandparents. The Canada Pension Plan (CPP) may be actuarially sound for the next 75 years — thanks to payroll tax hikes that have increased 201 per cent over the past two decades — but other schemes may not do so well. And given our lack of choice or ability to opt out of these government programs, Canadians are entirely dependent upon their government for key services like health care and retirement savings. But our government has proven itself to be very irresponsible and, at times, downright conniving. It is not a very good thing to be reliant upon. So, what happens if these programs fail?

Demographics

The chances of these programs failing will continue to increase thanks to the second feature of *generation screwed,* the demographic shift. Our population is aging. As baby boomers leave the workforce, they take much of their tax revenues with them and begin to consume more government services. Nine million Canadians are expected to leave the workforce over the next 20 years. That will cause a notable reduction in government revenues. But those revenues will be needed, as older Canadians are the largest driver of government spending. As the baby boomers start utilizing services like health care and old age benefits, and begin to collect from the CPP, our public finances will be put in further jeopardy. These entitlement programs will require more and more funding, from fewer and fewer taxpayers. This means inevitable tax hikes along with reduced government services down the road.

Debt

This increased demand in government services, coupled with a decreasing tax base, will lead to even more government borrowing, and exacerbate the final "D", government debt. Government debt is already a striking feature in our public finances. About ten per cent of all government spending goes towards paying interest on government debt, a figure that will worsen as interest rates go up. Politicians will have a choice as to how to pay for spending hikes in retirement benefits; they can either raise taxes or continue to borrow. The likely option will be to borrow, and this will drive future generations further into debt.

Combined government debt in Canada now exceeds $1 trillion. When you include future debt for government entitlement promises, the figure rises to $4.2 trillion, or almost two and a half times that of Canada's GDP. We are inching closer and closer towards the debt cliff we stood on in the early 1990s.

BIG PROMISES

"The American Republic will endure until the day Congress discovers that it can bribe the public with the public's money."

— Alexis de Tocqueville, *Democracy in America*

"Every election is a sort of advance auction sale of stolen goods."

— H. L. Mencken

All parents want their children to have a better life than they did. You probably hear this a lot. It's a terrible cliché, but it's completely true. Or at least, it's true of intentions. Parents make plenty of sacrifices, both economic and personal, and most work tremendously hard so that their children will have more opportunities and a better lot in life. But, as the saying goes, the road to hell is paved with good intentions, and much of what your parents have actually done is stolen from you.

This is jarring. What do I mean by this? Well, your parents and the baby boomers have built and perpetuated a political system that does not pay its bills. It relies on both borrowing and Ponzi schemes to give all people all the things they have been promised. Politicians sell big government programs and universal goodies without much thought of the sustainability of funding or the long-term prospects of paying the bills for these programs. Schemes like Social Security in the US or the Canada Pension Plan (CPP) here in Canada work so long as they constantly grow. They are built upon the assumption that those currently in the workforce will contribute enough into the system to pay for the benefits of current retirees. As each generation retires, new workers are added to the system so it constantly perpetuates itself. Many government entitlement programs are built on the premise of "pay-as-you-go" funding. There is never enough money in the accounts to pay out all the money promised. Just like any pyramid scheme or a multi-level marketing scam, our welfare system, specifically health care and pensions, rely on new people being added to the bottom to pay out to the people at the top.

Our parents and grandparents have made the assumption that young people want and will accept the system of government redistribution handed to them, and that the docile youth will simply agree to prop it up. By the time young people realize what a massive scam these government retribution schemes are, it will be too late. We will have already have already paid in significantly and therefore have a stake in perpetuating these Ponzi schemes, and dump them on the shoulders of the next generation. Thanks to this assumption, individuals cannot make simple choices about their financial investments, for instance deciding they don't want to use the CPP or our universal health care. There is no "opt out" option. We are forced to pay into these programs by design, and so will our children, grandchildren, and every future taxpayer until the programs inevitably go bankrupt. It's only fair, they say, since previous generations paid into these programs for decades without collecting benefits, on the premise that they would one day collect when younger generations took over.

Now, as they retire, it is your obligation to pay them.

This is the big promise. It is a new social contract derived between citizens and the state. The problem is that both parties have forged your signature, and now you are contractually obligated to pay their bills. The bigger problem is that the status quo is not sustainable (hence all the government debt), and is well along on the road to bankruptcy. But the first problem is that big promises, first made *to* baby boomers, then expanded *by* baby boomers, have left you with little choice about how most of your money will be spent for the rest of your life.

Short-term gain for long-term pain

Politicians and the political cycle are largely to blame. Alexis de Tocqueville noted this phenomenon when he studied and wrote extensively on the state of democracy in newly established America. The French philosopher and historian spent several years in the early 19th century studying the market revolution and burgeoning democracy in America, then published his magnum opus, *Democracy in America*, in 1835. Tocqueville was very complimentary of America's version democracy, which balanced the perception of equality with real liberty. He also warned that when politicians realize they have the power to spend public money as they please — essentially to bribe the people with their own money — they will do so, and this will lead to the erosion of democracy. We certainly observe this in the political cycle and elections today. Politicians and political parties make big promises to get elected. Those big promises are based on costly pledges that result in big spending.

During elections, politicians can, will and do say absolutely anything and everything necessary to get elected; they get into bidding wars with taxpayer money to woo voters.

We will build more hospitals! More schools! New subways! Jobs! Money for nothing!

As recent history proves, there is no shortage of bad ideas for politicians to ram down our throats during elections. Everything from Ontario's 2014 election promise to build a secondary CPP system on top of the current CPP, to Alberta's 2012 election pledge build 50 new hospitals, despite having recently built a "super hospital" in Calgary that was sitting empty because there were no funds to staff it.

After politicians use the election campaign to promise thousands of ways to spend imaginary money for you, the ones who win office will have to implement their policy platforms. That imaginary money becomes real taxes, and, more often than not, the costly promises far outweigh the original price tag. The promises outpace the funds actually collected in tax revenues. When politicians realize there is not enough revenue to pay all the bills, they are left with two choices: raise taxes or borrow.

Even big-government politicians now concede that raising taxes is deeply unpopular, and has problematic ripple effects throughout the economy. Borrowing has therefore become the all too easy choice. Most governments run deficits each year to finance spending growth, and take on additional debt to finance infrastructure. This is why governments across the West have racked up incomprehensible public debt. And remember, today's debt becomes tomorrow's taxes. Option two, borrowing, is simply a tax on the future. It's a tax on *generation screwed.*

Most politicians, both on the left and the right of the traditional political spectrum, enter into politics because they want to use government to fix problems and help people. This is a massive problem. Government is not a very effective source of solving personal problems. It usually just makes things worse, not only for those who bear the cost, but even for the supposed beneficiaries of government programs. Never trust a politician who says he or she want to make the government a force for good in people's lives. It means that politician wants the government to play a *larger* role in people's lives, and spend your money for you. These politicians imagine all the ways the government can run your life better than you can. Politicians either do not trust individuals to make good decisions ("good" as defined by those politicians), or they simply do not want people left to make their own decisions.

> "Of all tyrannies, a tyranny exercised for the good of its victims may be the most oppressive. It may be better to live under robber barons than under omnipotent busybodies. The robber baron's cruelty may sometimes sleep, his cupidity may at some point be satiated; but those who torment us for our own good will torment us without end for they do so with the approval of their own conscience."
>
> — C.S. Lewis, *God in the Dock: Essays on Theology and Ethics, 1979*

Most politicians and bureaucrats are, in fact, decent people, with honest intentions and big hearts. But that is the exact problem. Their hearts are bigger than their abilities and much bigger than their wallets. These individuals use their positions of power and authority to micromanage your life and your money. Regardless of their intentions, these "omnipotent busybodies" have driven us well down the road to bankruptcy, and eroded our liberty, sense of personal responsibility and independence in the process. Their intentions may be noble, but the result has been catastrophic.

And as governments offer more, individuals become reliant on their programs, and come to forget that they have the tools to take care of themselves without the help of those omnipotent busybodies. If the welfare state ended tomorrow, the country would go into shock. Canadians are not used to paying out of pocket for social services, and most would be financially and socially unprepared. We are not used to being free. But we were born to be free. Humans have lived relatively free lives for several centuries before the advent of the welfare state in the early to mid 20th century. Consider that that nearly half of all the money Canadians earn goes to government.

Imagine if our government, and therefore our tax burden, was massively reduced. Most working Canadians would have tens of thousands in additional take-home pay each year without government, which could be put into medical savings accounts and retirement investments. People would have the tools and the means, and eventually we would appreciate the restoration of our liberty. Schools and welfare programs could once again be run by private charities and churches (or mosques, synagogues, and temples), and individuals would no longer be forced to pay for programs that they personally oppose, or ones that are horrifically inefficient and wasteful.

As well-meaning as politicians may be, they are rapidly expanding the role of the government, and doing it at the expense of both our liberty and our finances. Coupled with the belief that government can help people, they hold a widespread belief that there isn't a problem that cannot be solved through more government. Aside from any objections on behalf of liberty, independence, freedom or skepticism towards the nanny state and the social impotency it brews, the very structure of big government is simply not affordable. It is reckless to pretend we can continue to expand the role of government and build new programs without additional funding (through higher taxes) and considering how those tax hikes will affect the economy.

Politics without romance

Politics is based on short-term calculations, instant gratification (many politicians even promise to implement their plans in the first 30 days!), and prolonging, deferring and ignoring any difficult decision until a future time not stated. This is especially true for decisions that may affect political approval ratings. Current administrations never talk about debt. They do not care about it; it will be up to future taxpayers and future politicians (likely a different political party) to deal with the mess they have created.

You may argue that most politicians have good intentions. Many conduct their job with honour and dignity, and respect the traditions of the office. It is unfair, therefore, to categorize an entire profession as being ruthless, selfish and irresponsible. But politics is based on trade-offs and calculations. Otto von Bismarck, the final president of the Prussian empire who oversaw the unification of Germany and became the first chancellor of the North German Confederation and then the German emperor in 1871, practiced what he called *realpolitik*. According to Bismarck, "politics is the art of the possible, the alternative — the art of the next best." Politics is a zero-sum game. With trade-offs come losers. And taxpayers lose when proponents of big government win.

In 1968, economist James Buchanan won the Nobel Prize in Economic Sciences for work on his Public Choice theory, an economic approach to politics that uses game theory to explore decision-making in the political arena. It assumes individual actors in politics are driven by the same motives as individuals in the economy. I had the opportunity to attend a lecture by Professor Buchanan at George Mason University in the fall of 2010. Public Choice is actually a very simple concept. Buchanan explained how people who are involved with government — politicians, bureaucrats, voters and special interest groups — are regular people with regular motives. They are not angels. They are not altruistic or disinterested. They are ordinary people that have ordinary motives. They aspire to achieve success, earn respect and improve their situation in life.

Just as we respond to incentives in the market, government officials also respond to incentives, and sometimes make decisions to better themselves at the expense of others. Politicians, at the end of the day, are just like everyone else; they are out for themselves. We shouldn't blame them for this. But we must acknowledge this simple fact. They are interested in self-preservation and winning elections. Public Choice theory demonstrates how a politician would therefore be willing to make deals with special interest groups that could benefit both parties but hurt the general public.

Just look at the political landscape across Canada. Some governments gladly hand out billions in raises and perks to unions. In exchange, those unions spend millions of dollars during election campaigns to flood the airways with negative attack ads against their political opponent. Unions help their favoured party win elections so those unions, in turn, will receive better contracts and more money for themselves. This *quid pro quo* comes at the expense of taxpayers, who are forced to pay the bill for rich union employee compensation. The general public pay for rich pensions that they themselves do not receive. These political parties and their union friends are willing to sacrifice the public good for their own personal gain.

Special interests win and leave taxpayers severely less well-off. The more we can imagine politics as a marketplace, the better we understand the wheeling and dealing that occurs. This takes the undeserved romanticism away from politics and calls a spade a spade. Even the most altruistic and caring activists are exposed as self-interested power brokers who will happily sacrifice your money in order to obtain some sort of power and influence for themselves and their coalition.

Politics is a marketplace just like the economy. Politicians "buy" votes by "selling" policies, ideas and promises. Unfortunately, everyone demands free stuff from the government and nobody wants to pay for it.

And as well-meaning as politicians can sometimes be, their hearts are bigger than their wallets, which is why they pry into yours. At the end of the day, it is a politician's job to get elected. That is their bottom line. Otherwise, they're out of a job and sustain humiliation and damaged earning potential. You should also keep in mind that behind every well-meaning politician is a team of cynical and ruthless political staffers, pollsters and lobbyists nudging them in the direction of poll-tested sound bites and targeted handouts to friendly stakeholders and valued interest groups.

Buchanan's Public Choice goes even further, to question the very purpose and ability of the government. While I might describe the role of government as protecting our liberties, others see the need for an activist government to respond to "market failures" and provide services that the market cannot sustain. But what is a market? If you boil it down, markets are simply a quick way to communicate complex information, based on people's choices and preferences (what someone may want to buy and how much they are willing to pay) and the availability of goods and services (communicated through prices). So, if a market fails in some certain area, how is a government any more likely to make it succeed? A bulky, unionized and bureaucratic government cannot better serve our needs than a swift and nimble marketplace made up of innovators, enterprisers and entrepreneurs who are driven by competition and hunger. This is why government initiatives fail much worse than so-called market failures.

So don't be fooled into thinking that somehow a benevolent government can solve the problems of our world and the market. The very premise of their worldview is flawed. Their big promises and solutions on how to fix the problem are just more of the same. Their solutions are nothing more than a misguided and distorted idea of how the world works: big promises are nothing but another tax on tomorrow.

James Buchanan took romance out of politics and his theory explains why cynicism and apathy are rampant in our evolved democracy. It is perfectly rational to be uninterested in politics; taxpayers ultimately lose, so why invest time on top of money? The chance of your vote actually mattering in the outcome of an election is next to nothing. The difference between the candidates and parties running for office is often marginal, at best. All politicians, to a varying degree, get into the business because they want a say in how your money is spent. Even the most fiscally prudent politicians have been known to spend wastefully and perpetuate our problems. So, what's the point of voting?

Politicians and governments should take low voter turnout and widespread apathy as a signal from the marketplace of citizens. People are not interested in politicians and their ideas or prescriptions. Instead of trying to force greater citizen involvement and political participation through forced quotas or new voting schemes, we should acknowledge this general disinterest and respect people's rational choice to be disinterested. Canadians don't generally like politics. They don't trust governments to solve real problems. Perhaps, people just want to be left alone. And this is as compelling a reason as any to limit the powers and abilities of government.

BIG SPENDING

"Economics is haunted by more fallacies than any other study known to man."

— Henry Hazlitt, *Economics in One Lesson*

"The ideas of economists and political philosophers, both when they are right and when they are wrong, are more powerful than is commonly understood. Indeed, the world is ruled by little else. Practical men, who believe themselves to be quite exempt from any intellectual influences, are usually slaves of some defunct economist."

— John Maynard Keynes

"Those who cannot remember the past are condemned to repeat it."

— George Santayana, Spanish philosopher

The previous chapter exposed how big promises by often well meaning but actually self-serving politicians equate to a massive price tag for you. Unless, of course, you are somehow part of a special interest group or union that drives the agenda, in which case, good for you. You are screwing over the rest of us, but good for you. This chapter will delve a little beyond big promises, which are not the only reason we have big spending; those promises are just the beginning of our troubles.

This chapter will explore the economic myths and fallacies that drive our ever-increasing public spending. Spending and debt-apologists in economics departments and financial journals across the country, around the world and throughout modern history are just as much to blame as the politicians making deals to win. Why? Because these economists give politicians a licence to spend your money! American satirist and political writer P.J. O'Rourke famously says "giving money and power to government is like giving whiskey and car keys to teenage boys." No kidding. Misguided economic fallacies are the bootleggers supplying our nation's teenage boys with whiskey and then giving them the keys to your car.

To get to the root of chronic over-spending in government, let's start with perhaps the most famous economic fallacy in circulation. In your high school Social Studies class, instead of learning about economics, household finances or, heaven forbid, some practical trade skills, you probably learned about *Black Tuesday* and the stock market crash of 1929 that spurred the Great Depression. Or so the myth goes. What would you say if I told you that there was no *Black Tuesday* and that the stock market crash is a myth? Totally made up. Yes, there was a lot of action on the *New York Stock Exchange* that week in October 1929, a lot of liquidation and stock sales. It was busy, but it was by no means a crash or the first day of the Great Depression. On Tuesday, October 29, 1929, the Dow Jones Industrial Average dropped a total of 30 points. As a point of reference, the stock market very regularly fluctuates by 30 points every single hour of everyday the NYSE is open. The story made the front page of Wednesday's New York Times, in a small headline on the side corner. And no one was calling it *Black Tuesday*. The headline read, "Stocks Collapse in 16,410,030-Share Day, But Rally at Close Cheers Brokers; Bankers Optimistic, to Continue Aid." Brokers cheering? Bankers optimistic? That doesn't sound so bad, does it?

You see, a stock market crash is an easy way to tell a complex story. The Great Depression was real, but its onset wasn't overnight. There was no *Black Tuesday*. The depression was not caused by a sudden, unpredictable crash caused by greed and markets. Capitalism and free markets are far from the culprit. But the lesson of this great myth taught to high school students around the world is that unfettered free market capitalism is the cause of economic hardship, and big government intervention is the solution. This is a lie. A lie packaged up and sold as propaganda to scare people and convince them that free markets shouldn't be left free.

Lawrence W. Reed of the *Foundation for Economic Education (FEE)* describes it as "the 20th century's greatest myth: [that] Capitalism and the free market economy were responsible for the Great Depression, and only government intervention brought about America's economic recovery." In Reed's pamphlet, "Great Myths of the Great Depression," he goes through the policies of both Presidents Herbert Hoover and Franklin D. Roosevelt, including FDR's disastrous New Deal, and the billions of dollars frittered away by the government in ongoing attempts to "jump start" the economy. FDR's massive expenditures — $10 billion at a time when tax revenues were $3 billion — caused the federal debt to skyrocket by 73 per cent over three years and led to massive tax hikes across the country, including FDR's wartime executive order for a 100 per cent tax on all income over $25,000.

The truth is, these policies merely prolonged the Depression and destroyed many businesses, households and livelihoods in the process. The myths surrounding the Depression allowed federal governments in both the US and Canada to seize new spending powers. It fostered the idea of mass government intervention in the economy and redistribution of wealth to "benefit working people". This was the beginning of the welfare state, justified at the time as a halfway point between free market capitalism emerging in the West, and growing government-centric communism, socialism, and fascism that were brewing in Europe and Asia.

We're all Keynesians!

The true story behind the Great Depression and its slow recovery is that chaos and fear in the marketplace — a marketplace that was heavily regulated and subsidized by the activist Hoover and FDR administrations — created a new opportunity for politicians and governments. This new idea was being championed by a wealthy English bureaucrat-turned-banker named John Maynard Keynes. Keynes argued that since the business cycle consists of ups and downs, there is a role for government in moderating this "boom and bust cycle." He called for state intervention during recessions and depressions to give jobs to the unemployed, utilize empty and abandoned factories, and bridge the economic gap between the recession and the recovery. Sounds pretty simple?

Perhaps in an abstract economic model, this may work. But real life is very different. To quickly fill gaps in an economy while transitioning towards a recovery would require mountains of money, unobtainable knowledge about future demand and overcoming imperfect information about the economy. A big, bureaucratic government cannot nimbly insert itself into the market, as much as Keynes and his followers may insist it can. The idea falls flat, on both its flawed premise and based on empirical evidence.

John Maynard Keynes is the father of modern day stimulus. He gave FDR and every successive politician a license to spend based on faulty logic, bad math and a lousy understanding of government. It is fitting that Keynes famously said, "in the long run, we're all dead." Keynesian economics is based on short-term thinking and reckless spending in the wake of an economic downturn. It calls for the government to engage in large scale spending and often printing money in an attempt to boost overall demand, create temporary construction jobs, and supposedly get the economy moving again. In reality, fake stimulus merely allows every politician to bring "pork" to their home ridings — that is, spend taxpayer money on new goodies for their constituents, like libraries, bridges, and even corporate welfare handouts to create temporary jobs. Or perhaps just reward campaign donors, but hey, it's all in the name of stimulus and therefore the public goes along with it.

Fake stimulus has very damaging effects that ring throughout the economy. When the government starts pumping stimulus money into the economy, businesses respond. They hire new workers. They buy new equipment. They expand their capabilities and their business to meet new demand. Governments send these false messages to businesses, encouraging them to grow and spend money, when they should be saving. Fake stimulus creates fake demand, and causes long ranging problems like artificial bubbles. But when the government stimulus spending ends, so too does the fake demand driving growth. Stimulus-receiving businesses often fail or lose their investment when their business model includes fake stimulus demand. Even worse for a economy is that this fake stimulus is fuelled by debt and borrowing. But why did we decide that a recession is a good time to start loading up the public credit card? Prior to FDR and the Great Depression, slow economic times would lead people to cut back, be modest with their spending, and work hard to create new opportunities. In modern day recessions, thanks to Keynes and his Keynesian successors, our politicians go on reckless spending sprees to boost their approval ratings, hand out cash to every program that will appease coalition votes, and saddle the people with unthinkable debt. Any economic stimulus spending is temporary. When government handouts stop, so too does the corresponding economic payoff. We stomach these bad economic policies during recessions, however, because we simply do not know what else to do. A politician who tells you to save and tighten your belt after a recession is never as popular as one who says "more money for everyone!" and begins to create new entitlement programs and handouts, not just for the poor and needy, but for everyone.

Keynes's idea of stimulus gave governments the moral justification to insert themselves into the economy in a way never previously imagined. His theories were quickly swept up and implemented by world leaders who were desperate to do something — anything — during a downturn. Instead of standing idly by while the economy slowly recovers, Keynes encouraged governments to act. Big mistake. Never give politicians the option to do more. They always will. They will spend your money to interfere with your life. Keynes himself was quickly elevated to celebrity status; especially in political circles where his work gave new enthusiasm to the role politicians could have in the economy. He was knighted in the UK in 1942 as the First Baron of Tilton, and given a seat in the House of Lords with the Liberal Party. He was also appointed chairman of the World Bank Commission and led the post-war negotiations that established the Bretton Woods fiscal agreements that have led the post-war era.

Contra Keynes

These new macroeconomic concepts may have been championed by the political elites of the time, but economists did not broadly accept them. In 1931, a young Friedrich Hayek challenged the work of Keynes in the journal *Economica,* questioning the basic formulas, definitions and arithmetic in Keynes's *Treatise on Money.* Keynes failed to answer very basic questions about his theory, and instead responded with his own criticisms of Hayek's work. This sparked a spirited debate of open letters and articles over the next 15 years, until Keynes's death. The two proposed very different responses to an economic crisis. Keynes called for government spending to counter fluctuations in the business cycle. Hayek warned of the damage caused by government interference, such as fake growth and the wasted economic opportunities lost from high taxes, as well as the need for more taxes to service government debt. The articles, personal correspondence and journal essays were collected and published by editor Bruce Caldwell in *Contra Keynes at Cambridge.* It is an excellent book for those wishing to see first-hand the arguments for and against modern-day Keynesian economics, from the original thinkers who gave us these ideas.

Keynesian spending is like the hair of the dog for a financial crisis. Instead of dealing with your hangover and temporarily suffering towards feeling better, Keynes tells you to skip the hangover altogether by drinking more. He tells you to engage in an ongoing binge. As university students may have already learned, this is not healthy and not a real solution. It merely prolongs that inevitable hangover, and makes it feel so much worse when it finally comes. And the hangover will eventually come. And thanks to these popular Keynesian policies, when the next generation of taxpayers are handed the bar tab, it isn't just for one big night out, it's for the entire binge.

Repeating history

Nobel Prize-winner and the 20th century's most prominent advocate of free markets Milton Friedman told an story that, in a nutshell, exposes what governments do to "create jobs" and "stimulate the economy." Friedman was in China in the 1960s, on a tour with a government official to witness the supposed economic growth at the time. The Chinese bureaucrat brought Friedman to a construction site where workers were building a new canal, and Friedman was shocked by what he saw. Instead of using modern tractors, backhoes, ploughs and steam engines, he only saw men using shovels. Friedman was taken aback. He asked why the workers were not using modern equipment, which would make the job faster and far easier. "You don't understand," replied the bureaucrat, "this is a jobs program." Friedman then responded, "I thought you were trying to build a canal. If it is just jobs you want, these workers should be using spoons, not shovels."

Sadly, the world repeated many of the same mistakes of the Great Depression again after the financial crisis in 2008. Again, government intervention in the market — this time through government-run mortgage agencies and government mandates to allow unqualified applicants to buy houses in the US — had led to volatility and chaos in the market. Again, the myth following the crisis was that:

1. The crisis was caused by greed and unregulated bankers, and;

2. We need government intervention to fix the problem.

Lies, lies, lies. The problem was actually caused by government and the "solution" of more government made the problem much, much worse. "Quantitative easing" — another way of saying "printing money" — has led to record consumer debt. Meanwhile, fake stimulus spending has driven governments deep into debt. America has 14-digit federal debt ($17 trillion and counting). This is why Ontario is now a have-not province. This is why supposed free market conservatives led by Stephen Harper brought in the largest spending budgets in Canadian history and put Canada's debt at record high. The myth of stimulus gave politicians permission to drive us into debt. No one listened to Hayek. Everyone listened to Keynes. When given the choice to do nothing or do something, to look meek and unprepared or champion new spending and look bold and in charge, politicians will always choose the latter. Especially when this brave face includes a blank cheque to build beyond their wildest dreams and win votes through targeted handouts and new infrastructure.

And when stimulus doesn't work? As it has not worked anywhere for anyone? Politicians go through withdrawal, and taxpayers are forced deeper and deeper into debt. Ending stimulus is the hardest part of the whole equation. Politicians know that when the gravy train dries up, so too does the "growth" they've stewarded in the economy. But many politicians sincerely believe they can solve all the problems of the economy, thanks to enabling economists like Keynes. Debt has become a tool that politicians use to spend their way out of a recession, without considering what debt really is. It is a tax on the future. A very costly tax, since it will be paid over and over, in both annual interest payments and eventually in paying down the principal.

As for a solution to get us out of the massive hole it has dug? Politicians essentially tell you to grab a spoon and keep digging.

BIG GOVERNMENT

"The natural progress of things is for liberty to yield, and government to gain ground."

— Thomas Jefferson

"Nothing is so permanent as a temporary government program."

— Milton Friedman

Big Promises + Big Spending = Big Government

The inevitable outcome of big promises made over time by politicians, and the big spending enabled by debt apologist economists, is a system of big government. On the one side, we have a welfare state that gives people the illusion that the state will take care of them, despite the uncomfortable fact that there is not enough money to cover the costs of these promises. Folks are lured into a false sense of security, and rely on the government to manage so much of our lives. We do this without ever double-checking the government's math or bank accounts. On the other side, and at the same time, politicians began to believe that government can and should interfere in the market place, to alter outcomes, avoid downturns and grow forever. Keynesian economists have given politicians a licence to spend money they don't have, and use it to pick winners and losers in the economy.

Both of these phenomenon cause governments to rack up incomprehensible debt levels. And *generation screwed* will soon inherit a mountain of debt from both comprehensive social welfare programs and failed government stimulus. The odds are against *generation screwed*. You have been born into a system of big government that doesn't pay its bills. This chapter will discuss the inherent flaws of big government; how it lures dependency and takes away choice, all the while digging us deeper and deeper into debt.

Years after the 2008 financial crisis, Prime Minister Stephen Harper talked about why Canada did so well during the global recession, relative to other western countries during that time. His government's "Economic Action Plan" featured only temporary spending injections and no permanent bureaucracies. Canada's federal government spent tens of billions of dollars — much of it borrowed — to give people the impression that the government was helping the economy. In reality, the money could have been spent digging ditches and filling them back in. It doesn't matter where the stimulus money goes, so long as it gets out the door with a news release. The reason why stimulus was more successful in Canada than other places is because it was not permanent. Stimulus was not used as a stealth way to expand the government, as was clearly done in such places as Quebec, Ontario and in the US federal government. And as Harper has explained, the rolling back of spending was as important as the initial rollout. In other words, the most important part of stimulus is *ending* stimulus. It is also the hardest part.

Scaling back government is one of the biggest challenges of modern day politics. That is because rolling back an entitlement program is near impossible. Once a government introduces a program that gives people stuff, they can never take that stuff away. Try to think of an example of just one government entitlement that has ever been taken away. It is very difficult to find a single example in Canadian history. That's the problem. By their very definition, people are "entitled to their entitlements." And it's only fair, since they have been forced to contribute to prop up these entitlement programs. This is why we have to fight the government every time it imagines a new hare-brained entitlement scheme, be it expanded government kindergarten or a new Ontario pension plan. Once it's in, it's in. Good luck taking it away. In the 2006 election, Stephen Harper literally bribed parents with their own money, by way of a new universal child care benefit that mails $100 cheques to all Canadian parents with young children, in order to avoid pressure to implement universal government daycare. It's a far better policy alternative to a new government bureaucracy, but a sad sign of the times that our government mails cheques to millionaires to avoid the inevitable growth of bureaucracy.

Milton Friedman once said that nothing is as permanent as a temporary tax. There are countless examples of never-ending "temporary taxes," from Britain's income tax, which was imposed as a wartime measure during the Napoleonic Wars (in 1799), to a 1.5-cent tax on gasoline introduced as a temporary deficit-reduction tax in Canada in the mid 90s. When the war ended, or the federal deficit was eliminated, the taxes remained. Big governments need big revenues to sustain all their big spending schemes. Governments have few sources of revenue aside from the power of taxation, so big governments rely on high taxes, stealth taxes hidden within the price of goods, or taxes introduced as a "temporary" measure. Just as people become dependent on big government, big government depends on the people's money. It is the government's lifeline.

Similarly, nothing is as permanent as a temporary spending program and nothing grows faster than a government bureaucracy. In 2011, the Harper government pledged, as part of its "Deficit-Reduction Action Plan," to cut five to ten per cent of each federal department. The result? After over a year of consultations and negotiations, the government finally implemented its plan. Or a meek version of it. After comprehensive spending reviews of all programs, some departments managed to rein in spending and hand out fewer cheques, but overall, spending still grew in the 2012 budget, and rose again in the 2013 budget. They cut about five per cent of government, but somehow also managed to grow spending! How did they pull this off? Well, the government needed to hire new personnel to implement the cuts. They needed to grow the bureaucracy in order to reduce and roll back spending.

Perhaps part of the reason bureaucracies always grow is because it is nearly impossible for a bureaucrat to lose their job. I was formerly the press secretary for a minister in the federal government, and I once had to deal with the issue of a mid-level bureaucrat who had been fired for spending "up to 100 per cent" of his time at work on "inappropriate websites." (If you are wondering what the inappropriate websites were, I will tell you that media sources at the time referred to this fellow as the "porno-crat.") Despite his poor workplace choices, the government was forced by a federal judge to give the porno-crat his job back. Why on earth would the federal judge make this ruling? Because the worker had received perfect reviews from his superior. Perfect reviews! The man spent all of his time at work creeping on inappropriate sites, and yet, he was considered a model employee. It must be easy to get perfect reviews if you are not required to do any work. Government employees doing no work receive perfect reviews because that is what is expected of them. They are hired to fill quotas or to give a middle manager more responsibility through more staff. But there is often absolutely nothing for them to do. And frankly, I'd rather bureaucrats be using inappropriate websites than finding new and creative ways to interfere in our lives. But even more so, I'd rather these redundant positions be eliminated. The ever-growing government is often underworked, so they often search for problems to solve. They constantly imagine new ways to insert the government into our lives. And once they design a new program, we get hooked on it, and come to depend on it.

More Government to Reduce Government?

Year after year, the government receives reports from the auditor general (AG), who is tasked with examining government programs and making recommendations on how to improve government services. But the AG is a government bureaucrat, self-interested in preserving the role of government in Canada. Most of the recommendations include hiring more people, increasing spending and giving the government more power over the lives of Canadians.

We expect such big things from offices like the Parliamentary Budgetary Office, the government Ombudsmen and the Auditor General. But they are often a huge disappointment to taxpayers. For instance, CTF's British Columbia director Jordan Bateman dug up details on BC's Auditor General for Local Government (AGLG), an office opened in 2012 under Premier Christy Clark with promises to clean up local government. But in the first two years since this office opened, only one report has been delivered. How much savings did it dig up? None. The report only focused on a $28,546 contract given to a company owned by a city employee. But it didn't really matter, since the city government no longer employed that one person.

A government office invented to save taxpayer money and make government more efficient has merely amounted to more waste of taxpayer money. On top of her annual salary of $199,316, the Auditor General for Local Government in BC was also given a $22,000 moving allowance and taxpayers shelled out another $57,000 to a headhunting agency that convinced her to move. On top of these expenses, this new office costs British Columbia taxpayers $2.6 million per year. And in the first two years, and nearly $5.3 million later, the AGLG has not saved taxpayers a red cent.

The very agencies designed to help address the problem of an ever-expanding government are a real part of the problem. Bureaucracies continue to grow, and as they do, they play a larger and larger role in our lives. We have moved beyond just the welfare state, in which every citizen has *access* to welfare, and into a welfare dependency trap, where everyone is *on* welfare, regardless of their wealth, status or ability to take care of themselves.

Wards of the State

As government employees cook up solutions in search of a problem, individuals become more and more reliant on the government. This is particularly the case for young people. Canadians have been conditioned to expect and rely on government handouts. We no longer think for ourselves, in ways once required of free citizens. We expect the government to think for us. Perhaps because our lives have been rather easy, compared to the vast majority of people around the world and throughout human history. We have grown up and lived in an extraordinary time, both peaceful and prosperous. We are not properly equipped to be individual, self-reliant, grown-ups.

We do not save. We spend. And then we expect the government to subsidize our education, pay for our health care, and save for our retirement, not to mention subsidize our commute to work on public transit, give us employment insurance, bail out our employers if needed, and heck, even raise the nation's children while their parents are at work. The more the government does for us, the more we rely on government. It is a vicious cycle.

Think about your life so far. You were born in a government hospital surrounded by government-employed doctors and nurses. Your parents brought you to subsidized or state-owned day cares, community centres and libraries. You likely attended a government school and were taught a government curriculum by unionized government teachers. Now, if you attend a Canadian university, chances are it is state-owned and your tuition is highly subsidized by taxpayers. If you have a student loan, it is underwritten and guaranteed by taxpayers.

You have received a tremendous amount of government help, and you may have a positive impression of your interactions with these government programs. Certainly you cannot imagine life without them. You are hooked on the government. They have lured you in. Now you are an addict. Addicted to big government. This means you are likely willing to accept the role of big government and not put up much of a fight as it continues to grow, and as you reach an age where you stop receiving and start paying in. You will simply fork over more and more money without protest or even much thought. This works out well for the government, which, after all, desperately needs your money. They need you to pay into their system. And now that you've been lured in, you are about to spend the next 50 years or more contributing far more than you will ever get back.

Universal everything

The role of the government has drastically changed over the last hundred years. It hasn't always been the case that the government was in charge of so many aspects of an individual's life in Canada. We are currently experiencing the welfare state gone wild. The welfare state was slowly introduced during the Great Depression, as a compromise between free market capitalism and planned-economy communism. Capitalism was problematic; given that part of its structure is that some people fail while others succeed. The system relies on the failure as much as the success. Businesses fail because they do not understand their customers; they fail to innovate or provide a product or service that people are willing to pay for. This is a good thing, especially for consumers who are constantly offered a better service and a more competitive price. It is not good, however, for the individual business owner who fails to understand his customer's needs. The welfare state was designed to help those who fail in the market, and do not have the skills or abilities to make a living on their own. The basic social safety net was designed to help provide a basic minimum standard of living for everyone in society — regardless of their background or abilities.

But the welfare state has morphed. It has expanded far beyond just providing a minimum standard of living for the very poor. Universal access to private institutions soon led to free goodies and state takeovers. The government doesn't just ensure that everyone has access to health care and education; they own and administer the services through government monopolies. The welfare state isn't just there to protect the weakest and most vulnerable from the realities of the marketplace. It is there to give free stuff to everyone, and protect everyone from themselves. Programs have been expanded to take care of people who have good jobs and could easily take care of themselves. Our universal government programs are now so expansive they give money to everyone. Middle and upper-income earners included. Canadian citizenship comes with a lifetime supply of government cheques, whether you need them or not.

And government pits us against our fellow citizens. The government trough becomes a tragedy of the commons; everyone competes for the handouts from government redistribution. Government resources are finite. And government promises are bigger than government revenues. It is therefore in the best interest of every individual to take as many resources as possible from the government. But those limited resources are depleting. So each citizen is pitted against one another to maximize their own handouts, at the expense of everyone else. Just like the original tragedy of the commons (the collective property known as "the commons" in 19th century Britain that was depleted by over-harvesting by competing farmers who had no incentive to share or leave any resources for others) our government has become a tragedy of the commons for individual receivers. Everyone will over harvest until everything is gone. Without individual ownership it is just a matter of time before the scarce resources will deplete; and there will be nothing left for anyone.

Democracy's Fatal Conceit

Instead of a welfare state designed to help those who fall through the cracks, our system has been transformed into a welfare trap society. The majority of spending from our government goes to the vast middle class through entitlement programs. These entitlement programs are funded by everyone, and therefore expected by everyone. They are politically untouchable, since everyone has a stake in fighting to keep what is owed to them. And because no government entitlement program ever gets rolled back once it has been introduced, we are stuck with them. Even when we cannot afford them and they are driving us deep into debt.

This is a crisis of big government. How can we pay for so many people to receive such expansive social entitlement programs when more people are collecting than those paying in? The government has chronically overextended itself, and the welfare state is yet another ticking time bomb in public finances.

PART II

YOUR PROBLEM

"Mom & Dad partied and left you with the bill!"

— Troy Lanigan, CTF President

"How did you go bankrupt?"
"Two ways. Gradually, then suddenly."

— Ernest Hemingway, *The Sun Also Rises*

The problem of big government is a burden we all have to bear. That's the bad news. Well, it's the beginning of the bad news — and there is a lot of it. The costs associated with big government are all working against *generation screwed*. The burden to pay will soon fall on your shoulders. And these costs will be higher than ever before, thanks to another phenomenon that is working against you: the demographic shift. Your generation is uniquely screwed because of the demographic changes that are occurring as the largest generation, the baby boomers, is retiring from the workforce and aging into poor health.

The baby boomers are a unique generation. They grew up in an era of sustained peace and economic growth, and because of this good fortune, they became the wealthiest cohort in human history. Unfortunately for *generation screwed*, they will likely remain the wealthiest generation in human history. This is because wealth creation seems to have reached a plateau; meanwhile, your government burden is higher than ever before. We are no longer growing. Declining fertility rates among baby boomers and subsequent generations means our natural population is contracting. Immigration as a policy tool is useful in helping to fill in this gap, but it will not be enough to lift us back to the levels needed to sustain big government spending and fulfill all the promises of the baby boomer generation.

As our population growth slowed, so too did economic growth. Many in *generation screwed* have already experienced economic hardship, after graduating into a financial recession with dim career prospects and few opportunities. But what if it wasn't a recession? What if this is the new normal? Bad policies have contributed to anemic growth and record high youth unemployment. Until we establish why this problem persists, it won't simply be solved by more subsidies or another real estate bubble.

The pending retirement of the baby boomers will open Pandora's box. As this very large generation begins to age, they will ease into retirement, receiving generous pensions and free unlimited health care courtesy of the taxpayer. Meanwhile, *generation screwed* will be forced to pick up the tab. Not only are baby boomers retiring early, they are also living longer than ever. This is a great achievement of our time, as modern medicine allows us to live long and healthy lives. But the big government model was designed when people were not living as long. Originally, pensions were designed to help citizens with added benefits for four or five years after retirement. The math worked because the economy was booming and the growing population easily supported the costs of retirement pensions for a few short years. But demographics have shifted significantly, and public policy has not course-adjusted. People now live for decades after retirement, and expect the same extensive social benefits that were designed in a different era. Simply put, we are not rich enough to pay for everyone in society to live for decades after retirement on the government dole.

Our welfare state was built upon assumptions about growth that have not panned out. And thanks to these miscalculations, we are slowly heading towards bankruptcy. The welfare state is an illusion, and it is fuelled by debt. It may survive long enough to fulfill the baby boomers' illusion, but it will certainly leave *generation screwed* debt-ridden.

Virtuous Canada

Don't get me wrong, Canada is an extraordinary country and Canadians are incredibly fortunate people. We live in a remarkable place and in interesting times. Any Canadian can achieve success, happiness, acceptance and freedom. We celebrate our diversity and our achievements, while always fighting for what is right. We have inherited a wonderful country.

Growing up in Vancouver, I remember being told that being a Canadian was like winning the lottery. Vancouverites take pride in living in the best place on earth, but admit it isn't just the natural beauty that makes it so remarkable. Canada is a special place. The world we know here at home is very different from that of the vast majority of the people in this world. None are as lucky. Whether you were born here or immigrated, whether you're a Haligonian or an Edmontonian, life is good in Canada, and Canadians live well.

There is nothing, however, inherently virtuous about being born somewhere; we live the good life because of what has been fought for and achieved here in Canada. Older generations are to thank for our freedom. The men and women who sacrificed their lives and their liberty did so to ensure the world is free and peaceful for us, the future generations of Canadians. They have handed us a remarkable country that is not only free and peaceful, but also prosperous beyond their wildest dreams. We live in a remarkable time and place in history, and each of us has a duty to remember how we got here.

But just as young Canadians did not personally fight against fascism and communism in Europe and around the world, and are mere beneficiaries of that sacrifice, we also did not personally consent to the endless government entitlement programs that politicians signed us up for before we were born. Many brave individuals fought for and achieved our free society, while many others sold away our financial future. Big promises by older generations will leave this one — *generation screwed* — with big bills to pay.

BABY BOOMERS

To understand why you are *generation screwed* you should first understand the baby boomers. While they are not the architects of the welfare state, and your problems are not entirely their fault, they are an important player in the story of why you are screwed. And it will be their mass retirement that exposes the major fault lines of Canada's big government.

Baby boomers are just that: members of the baby boom that occurred after the Second World War. Starting in 1946, Canadian parents started having lots and lots of babies. The birth rate jumped from fewer than 200,000 per year in the 1930s and early 40s, up to 400,000 in the early 50s, and up to 500,000 in the early 60s. But the boom didn't last, and by the 70s, the birth rate in Canada was back down to a sustained average of about 350,000 per year.

Number of Births in Canada by Year

Source: Statistics Canada. Figures for Fertility Overview 2008. Figure 1 Births in Canada 1926 to 2008. Publication 91 – 209 X

The nearly 20-year surge is the baby boom — the large generation of post-war babies born between 1946 and 1964. This population surge came alongside massive post-war economic growth and wealth creation. The war had not brought the West out of the great depression. The post-war period of peace and stability, alongside the fertility rate surge, brought about a large increase in labour and productivity. Able-bodied young men and women were no longer fighting in the war; they were home and eager to build a business, have a family and live the American (and Canadian) Dream. Baby boomers were the beneficiaries of this growth and this wealth. North America became the richest place on the planet; the vast middle class grew out of poverty and was offered new opportunities never before imagined. The post-war era of prosperity is certainly something worth celebrating. But along with economic growth, came government growth.

Alongside high wages and more wealth in Canada, came more demands for government imposed minimum services and expanded social entitlement programs. The first government hospitals were opened in Canada at the provincial level in Saskatchewan (1946) and Alberta (1950). By 1957, health care in Canada had been nationalized. As the welfare state expanded, government pensions were introduced first with the Old Age Security benefit (1952) and the Canada Pension Plan (1966). The welfare state expanded beyond anyone's expectation. Even original pioneers for the welfare state, activist Beatrice Webb in England for example, wouldn't be able to imagine all the things the government now controls and doles out. During the past several decades, sneaky politicians (and even sneakier bureaucrats) have found new and creative ways to both expand government programs and finance them.

And at the time, we could nominally afford it. These plans were all designed in an era with a booming economy and what appeared to be never-ending growth. With newfound wealth and prosperity in Canada, it is easy to imagine how politicians of the day thought the boom would never end. They certainly designed these programs on assumptions of constant economic and population growth.

Most of the assumptions about the welfare state, and our ability to pay for such a big government, were based on calculations that were true in the post-war era. But the surge in the population — through both high fertility rates and immigration — and the booming economy were not permanent fixtures. As it turned out, the baby boom was an anomaly. And while our population and the economy are no longer growing as rapidly as during the baby boom, we are spending as if we were. This growth stopped in the 1970s, but Canadian leaders ignored facts, and used borrowing and debt to uphold the mirage.

As this debt-fuelled growth continues, fewer taxpayers are responsible for a larger burden. Instead of the costs of the welfare state being spread out across a generation that produced 500,000 births per year, we are spreading them across a cohort half that size. And baby boomers aren't just living one or two extra years after retirement; they are tripling and quadrupling typical life expectancy after retirement. *Generation screwed's* proportionate government burden, therefore, is much larger.

This problem is not unique to young Canadians. Young people across Europe and the United States are in a similarly unlucky position, with aging populations and exploding social welfare spending. Europe was once championed by intellectuals and academics around the world for their charitable and egalitarian welfare entitlements. But as EU countries such as Greece, Portugal, Spain and Italy also struggle to make their loan payments, meanwhile culture and religious-wars are erupting on the streets in many European capitals and France flirts with a 75 per cent taxation rate, I'm not sure these societies are any longer heralded for their enlightenment. Europe has become just another region of basket case economies.

While Canada is sometimes dismissed as a socialist bastion compared to our freedom loving neighbours to the south, Canada is actually in a slightly better positioned than the US to meet the challenges of *generation screwed.* Canada now scores significantly better than the US in Economic Freedom of the World reports, which measures the following factors:

- Size of government: expenditures, taxes & state-owned enterprises

- Legal structure & property taxes

- Access to sound money

- Free trade measures like tariffs and barriers

- Regulation of credit, labour unions, and businesses

Based on these measures, Canada has greater economic freedom than the US. Similarly, in the Economic Freedom of North America index, Alberta and Saskatchewan top the list as the freest jurisdictions. And while our debt is daunting, it is only a fraction of that in the Land of the Free.

There is another reason Canada is better positioned to reform our welfare state and manage expectations about a post-welfare government. We have been here before. Baby boomers encountered early warning signs of our unsustainable big government problems in the early 1990s. They were forced to deal with decades of government growth that outpaced economic growth, and made the Canadian government resemble modern-day Greece.

And because Canadian politicians in the early 1990s avoided potential catastrophe, their reforms put Canada in an excellent position to weather the storm of the great recession in 2008, and provide something of a roadmap for indebted governments to turn around their finances.

The shortfalls that paved the way for *generation screwed* were plainly there for anyone to observe. After rapid and monumental government growth in the 1970s, borrowing and debt soared during the 1980s and early 90s. Interest on the debt became the single largest expense in the budget, taking up 36 cents of every tax dollar spent. Then-Prime Minister Jean Chrétien and his finance minister Paul Martin were left with no choice; they froze all spending and implemented deep cuts to every department. Modest tax hikes were also part of the plan to balance the books, but according to Paul Martin at the 2014 World Taxpayer's Conference in Vancouver, "the government had a spending problem," not a revenue problem. The ratio of spending cuts to tax hikes was seven to one.

Between the 1994-95 and 1998-99 budgets, federal program spending fell by 12 per cent, making it possible for the government to balance the budget by 1997, run surplus budgets for over a decade, and pay down over $100 billion of the federal debt.

Federal Budget Deficits ($ billions)

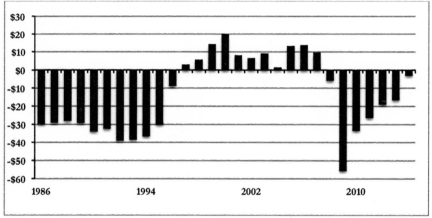

Source: Government of Canada. Archived Fiscal Reference Tables, Ministry of Finance.

Chrétien and Martin accomplished something rare and truly remarkable, and it certainly was not easy. They were able to accomplish this change politically because they argued it was the only way to save Canada's coveted entitlement programs. In order to ensure the future of the welfare state, they needed to ensure a fiscally healthy government. In order to be generous with other people's money, they needed to ensure the short-term sustainability of big government and therefore needed to be fiscally responsible. They accomplished their goals. But unfortunately, the problem was not solved. Chrétien and company addressed the symptoms — spending and deficits — but the underlying sickness wasn't cured. And today, the disease of big government and mass dependency on big government is metastasizing. The plague will continue until we find the courage to fight the disease itself, or until the cancer spreads and eventually triumphs.

The baby boomers encountered a spending scenario similar to what *generation screwed* will inherit, but instead of fixing the imbalance and finding an affordable and sustainable model, the baby boomers fixed things only enough to kick the can down the road to *generation screwed*. The welfare state continues to expand. These reforms were mere tweaks to government entitlements to make them affordable in the short to medium-term. But they didn't bother to fix the problem for future generations.

Baby boomers were born into the most prosperous era in history, and in many ways, they took it for granted. They trusted and believed all the promises of all the politicians, and enabled massive growth in massively unsustainable programs.

MASS RETIREMENT

Baby boomers are typically defined as individuals born in the 1940s, 50s and 60s. The average retirement age in Canada is 62, so simple math tells us that baby boomers started to retire in the early 2000s and will continue to retire en masse until the late 2020s. This exodus from the workforce will be a millstone around the neck of *generation screwed.* As more people retire, fewer remain in the workforce to pay taxes and fund government programs. The first demographic problem we will encounter is the hit to the government's income. The second is that retired baby boomers will use ever more government services, and as they age, their welfare programs will become more and more expensive.

The structure of the welfare state requires robbing Peter to pay Paul. But what happens when Peter retires?

Part of the problem is that the government has not saved enough for this coming demographic shift. Programs are not pre-funded, and many are already facing shortfalls. The funding equations for these programs assume that every generation is the same size and revenue growth will remain constant. But this is no longer the case. This chapter examines the mass retirement of baby boomers, their shift from net-contributing taxpayers to net-collectors, and the disastrous effect this will have on the government's ability to remain solvent.

Our big government welfare state system has generally worked over the past half-century. This is because of constant growth, in both the population and the economy. The system is sustainable so long as there are enough people contributing to government coffers to pay for all those who are collecting government entitlements. Constant growth drives the affordability of our government, and the gaps are filled by borrowing and debt.

But things are about to change. Nine million baby boomers are due to retire from the workforce over the next 20 years, swapping sides in the government's math equation. As these folks retire, the percentage of the population over the age of 65 will continue to soar. More people will be retired and collecting government entitlements, and less will be net-contributing taxpayers to fund the government coffers. Currently, government spending per citizen over the age of 65 is a remarkable $45,000 per year. This comes regardless of other factors, such as their income or net worth. In fact, 42 per cent of millionaires in Canada are over the age of 65, and even these folks receive about $45,000 per year directed from taxpayers!

By the time I may retire, about one quarter of the population will be over the age of 65, and the burden for paying retirement benefits will fall on an incredibly small number of shoulders. The effect on our books will be catastrophic.

Per Cent of Canada's Population Over 65

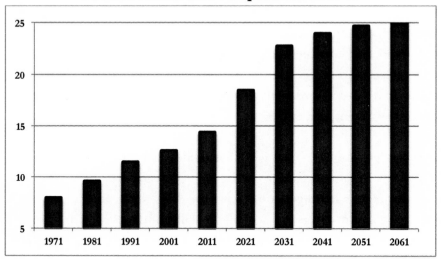

Source: Government of Canada, Canadians in Context – Aging Population, Ministry of Employment and Social Development Canada.

Another way to grasp the effect of baby boomer retirement is to consider the ratio of working age Canadians to retirees. In 1971, there were 7.8 people between the ages of 15 and 64 for every one over the age of 65. In that scenario, it is reasonable to assume that the taxes of nearly eight workers could handily support the one retiree through their final few years of life. But by 2010, the number of workers per retiree had shrunk to 5.4. Those five individuals are forced to carry a larger burden for the retirement needs of that one individual. Each working person only has four other taxpayers to share the cost, as opposed to the seven others in the 1970s. In 2012, the ratio of working-age to retirement-age workers fell again, to 4.6 to 1. In 2020, it is projected to shrink to 3.5, and then again to 2.7 by 2030. By 2040, when I will be getting close to retirement age, there will only be 2.5 workers left in the workforce for every one over the age of 65.

Ratio of Workers to Retirees

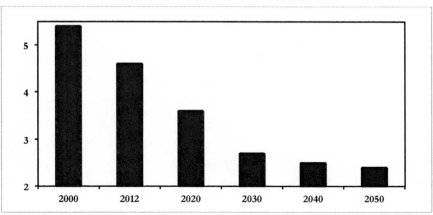

Source: Statistics Canada. Demography and the labour market, from "Demographic and Economic Perspectives from 2000 to 2050."

You can imagine the increased tax burden necessary for those 2.5 workers to pay for all the social welfare benefits promised to each retiree. And as we know not everyone who is of age to be in the workforce is actually a net taxpayer. Very few Canadians join the workforce as a full-time worker at age 15. The country is better for this; as most Canadians graduate from high school, and most go on to receive some post-secondary education or training. But it simply cuts into that worker ratio, making it even more severe. The typical Canadian doesn't actually join the full-time workforce until their early to mid or, increasingly, their late-twenties.

The picture gets even darker when we take into consideration the fact that not everyone works. Not every Canadian is a taxpayer. The total employment rate in Canada is about 61 per cent of the total population. Furthermore, about 21 per cent are on a government payroll. Government workers do pay taxes; however, their salaries are comprised of tax dollars, so they are not net-contributors to the system.

Back to the ratio: when the worker-to-retiree ratio drops to 2.5, the real ratio will be much lower. Because about ten per cent are still in school, 40 per cent are not in the workforce and 20 per cent work for the government, the real ratio of net taxpayers to retirees will be more like 1.2 to 1. There will be a nearly equal number of retirees and net-contributing taxpayers. *One taxpayer for every single retiree.*

You can start to see how there is simply no way that *generation screwed* will be able to afford this tab. There is no way we will receive the same retirement benefits and entitlement programs as what is received by Canadian retirees today. You are paying for other people to have a richer retirement than you will have.

In all likelihood, Canada's lucrative elderly benefits and programs will not survive. Canada's welfare state will either have to be drastically scaled back or it will collapse. Either way, Canadians will experience significant cuts to their social programs and social handouts. The important task for future politicians will be to manage expectations and draw people away from government dependency. You were forced to pay into the system for years, but your money went to fund retirement programs for baby boomers, not for yourself. These retirement programs will not exist when you retire.

Flipping the Population Pyramid

The problem is not that population growth has not kept up with assumptions made by the designers of these welfare programs. The problem is the massive expansion of the welfare state in the first place. This is the problem in and of itself, and the fact that the government can no longer afford to pay its bills is just the ugly reality of the welfare state. It is a system of government that makes everyone dependent on other peoples' money. As long as a society is experiencing constant growth, in both fertility and wealth creation, it can generally sustain lucrative handouts and promises to elderly citizens. But this house of cards begins to shake when we stop growing. And the population in Canada did stop growing after the baby boom. As these baby boomers age, there will not be enough people at the bottom to carry the weight of all the people at the top. Just like any Ponzi scheme or multi-level marketing scam, collapse comes when not enough new people join the scheme. Combine decades of declining fertility rates with the mass retirement of baby boomers and the cards come tumbling down.

Canada's Population Pyramid 1960 vs. 2000

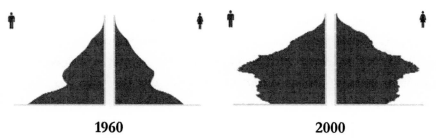

1960   **2000**

Source: Statistics Canada, Historical Age Pyramid. Census of population and Population Estimates Program, 1921 to 2011.

The above is a population pyramid for Canada in both 1960 — the height of the baby boom — compared with Canada in 2000. The bottom of the axis are new born babies, and each vertical line in the pyramid represents an age and the number of people alive born in that year, with men on the left and women on the right. In growing economies, such as Canada's in the 1960s, there are enough young and working age people to easily support the elderly people (represented at top of the pyramid) who may need extra care from the government and taxpayers. But when you look at our population distribution in 2000, the bulk of the population is middle-aged. The newer generations are increasingly smaller. This is not good news for social entitlement programs, which rely on the working-aged population to prop up. As the largest cohort in society ages, our bills are going to go through the roof.

The mass exodus of baby boomers from our workforce will threaten our public books; early retirement makes the problem even worse. In Ontario, according to the Ontario Teachers' Pension Plan, the typical teacher retires at age 59, after working for 26 years, and then collects a defined-benefit pension for 31 years. These are the kinds of contracts and deals that can only be negotiated with an employer who has no concept of affordability and no grasp of economic realities. Not to knock individual teachers — who *wouldn't* take this deal if offered? — but the governments who negotiate these deals and the unions that push for ever-higher pay and ever-higher pensions ought to be held accountable for these truly reckless promises. Nobody should expect to retire at age 59 and collect nearly a full salary, indexed to inflation, from taxpayers until the day they die. You will soon be paying for baby boomers to retire earlier than ever, collect more lucrative retirement benefits than ever, and live and therefore collect longer than ever.

Ontario teachers may be a particularly egregious exception, but the concept of retiring in your 50s is a real expectation for many. The typical government employee in Canada retires at age 58 and collects a lucrative, taxpayer-funded pension for more than 20 years!

Average Life Expectancy vs. Government Benefits

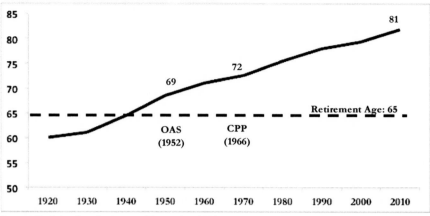

Source: Statistics Canada. Accessed September 2014.

While the set retirement age in Canada is 65, the typical Canadian now retires at age 62. Meanwhile, life expectancy in Canada has soared to 81 years old. Our country's old age entitlement programs were designed and created under totally different circumstances. The Old Age Security (OAS) benefit program was introduced in 1952, at a time when life expectancy was 69 years. The program was designed to give seniors a benefit for approximately four years after retirement. The Canada Pension Plan was similarly introduced in 1966 when the typical Canadian lived to age 72. Things have changed, and Canadians now live longer and therefore collecting very expensive government benefits for longer. This comes at a significant expense to the taxpayers.

Canadians are now spending 20 years at the end of their lives out of the workforce and draining from government coffers. Not only is this unaffordable, it's a shame. Many of these people could still be productive, helpful and happy in the economy. Many seniors are not happy to retire, and many suffer from depression after leaving the jobs they've worked so hard to achieve. But they leave the workforce because it doesn't make financial sense for them to stay. So the real question is, why do our governments provide incentives for folks to leave the workforce? Why does our society encourage any retirement, let alone early retirement? It shouldn't.

And other things have changed. When these retirement benefit programs were created, seniors were some of the poorest and most vulnerable members of society. Even in 1970, a reported 40 per cent of Canadian seniors lived in poverty. But things have drastically changed. Today, the number of seniors in poverty is less than five per cent — about half the rate among the population as a whole.

Seniors are now nine times richer than their Millennial grandchildren and members of *generation screwed*. The highest income group in Canada are folks between the age 55 and 64, followed by seniors over the age of 65. The net worth of seniors continues to grow, and everything from real estate prices to tax benefits and government redistribution has contributed to the growth in the riches of seniors. In fact, in combined government benefits and tax breaks, taxpayers pay $45,000 a year per senior in Canada![2]

This is why it makes no sense for governments to continue to funnel money from younger and poorer workers to wealthy seniors. There is an elderly bias in our tax system and with government entitlements that ought to be reversed.

But there is a significant force at play that prevents an honest discussion about this government redistribution from poorer young Canadians to richer seniors. As discussed in Part I of this book on Public Choice economics, politicians aim to please, and will only suggest and discuss policies that will help them get re-elected. Seniors

---

[2] Maclean's Magazine, "Old and Loaded." September 15, 2014.

are a powerful voting block in society. They can be counted on to show up to the polls and vote in large numbers. We also know that baby boomers are the largest cohort in our population, and in a democracy where the majority rules, they will rule.

These baby boomers and seniors are self-interested. They will therefore continue to vote for politicians who promise them the best deal. They will not vote to roll back their own entitlements or scale back their privilege, even if it comes at the expense of their children and grandchildren. They believe they are entitled to this treatment.

Young people, on the other hand, don't typically vote. Many who will be the most screwed by these policies are still too young to vote. *Generation screwed* is not a significant voting block or interest group, so politicians are not really listening to their concerns. Seniors will continue to vote themselves bigger cheques and better deals, while young Canadians and future taxpayers have no say whatsoever. The joys of democracy.

END OF GROWTH

You will likely graduate from university with a significant debt load. This is arguably because you were sold a false bill of goods about your future prospects, job opportunities and the value of an education. Or perhaps you're in debt because you enjoyed school so much that you spent too much time there and not enough time working and earning. Regardless, it is not your fault that you will graduate into a prolonged recession. Debt burdens are scary, and it is a bleak outlook knowing the first decade of your career will be spent making debt payments and not enjoying your 20s the way you'd hoped.

Student debt is a burden you will overcome. Government debt, on the other hand, I'm not so sure about. You are on the hook for big government and endless welfare-state programs, and will pay higher premiums and taxes despite the likelihood that you will never collect the benefits. This is an ugly combination. *Generation screwed* faces a future with limited economic growth and fewer opportunities than previous generations. The economy is not growing, so you will likely make less money too. Regardless, you will still be forced to pay more to the government in taxes. This chapter describes how student debt is the least of your debt concerns, the enduring 2008 recession and its reactionary protest movements and how our economy stopped growing.

Some mainstream observers like the CBC have started to assign
Millennials, those born roughly between 1982 and 2004, the new
nickname "generation screwed." This generation has been described
— and in some ways written off — as entitled, arrogant, unambitious
and even narcissistic. Raised by baby boomer parents, this generation
had big expectations and came to believe that things would come
easy. Graduating into a recession has been a dose of harsh reality,
and it was certainly a wakeup call to many. No one expects to
graduate university with record debt and then enter into a workforce
record high unemployment levels. The unemployment rate for
Canadians aged 15 to 24 — that is people who are actively looking
for work but cannot find a job — remains stubbornly at nearly 14 per
cent over the past few years. Compare this with the general Canadian
unemployment rate of folks aged 25 to 54: 5.7 per cent.

Flat Wages in Canada

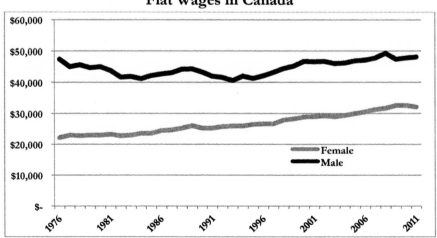

Source: Statistics Canada. Table 202-0102 – Average female and male earnings, and female-to-male
earnings ratio, constant dollars, annual. Accessed September 2014.

Even more depressing is the trend of stagnant wages. Once young

Canadians finally do find work, they can expect to earn less, in inflation-adjusted dollars, than past generations. While women have gradually seen an increase in their wage — a result largely from the sheer quantity of women entering the workforce in general — male wages are about what they were in 1976. We are no longer getting richer with each generation. We have reached a plateau, and *Generation screwed* will earn less money than our parents.

The economy has refused to recover during the past few years. That's because this is not your average recession. It is a prolonged recession that was partially caused by government, and then made worse by government intervention.

As distinct as Canadians believe themselves to be from our American neighbours, our economies are closely intertwined. We are the world's largest trading partners, importing and exporting over $500 billion per year and making up three-quarters of Canada's overall exports and three-fifths of our total imports. When the US struggles, Canada feels the effects. And while our banking norms prevented the same kind of financial crises experienced in the US in 2008 and 2009, we fell into a recession nonetheless. And when the US government responded by opening the floodgate of economic stimulus spending and handouts, Canada followed suit.

Bailouts and the Protestors

In one of his very last moves as US President, George W. Bush ordered the *Troubled Asset Relief Program* (TARP), a plan to hand out over $700 billion in corporate bailouts to companies with "troubled assets." Approximately $430 billion in TARP money has made it out the door; a staggering amount of money to take out of the economy during a recession to distribute to failing companies. The TARP funds came from a combination of taxes and borrowing. The government took money away from successful companies, and passed it over to risky, failed, faulty and even corrupt companies. And it brought on two significant protest movements in the late 2000s and early 2010s. The *Occupy Wall Street* movement and the *Tea Party*. Both groups were essentially protesting the same thing, although they were painted in two very different lights.

The Tea Party protesters were enraged with the economic policies of the US, the waste of tax dollars and disrespect to taxpayers. It may be pointless to try to defend the Tea Party movement to Canadians who, especially in Central Canada, pounce on every opportunity to stick up their noses and look down on our American neighbours. Emily Etkins, a PhD student at UCLA, chronicled the libertarian roots of the Tea Party movement, and in a quantitative study, found that the vast majority of these protestors were motivated by economic complaints. More than half of the signs at one rally demanded smaller government, including such topics as the role of government, taxes, spending, the deficit and concerns about socialism. There were negative and ugly messages at these rallies as well, which is what the media chronicled and focused on. But, in fact, only a quarter of the signs reflected direct anger at Barack Obama and less than five per cent mentioned his religion or ethnicity. The racially charged undertones highlighted by the media reflected the fringe of these rallies; the primary motivating factor was the growing size of government and the economic mismanagement of taxpayer dollars exemplified through the TARP bailouts.

The Occupy Wall Street (OWS) movement was a similar, citizen-led advocacy movement to protest the financial institutions on Wall Street, particularly those that received TARP funds. It is ironic that protestors blamed bankers for *receiving* taxpayer-funded bailouts, but did not seem to blame the federal government for *giving* them.

Regardless, in the autumn of 2011, these protests occupied lower Manhattan. Subsequent squatters "occupied" downtown parks in cities across North America and Europe. OWS was protesting against the rich, and what they perceive as greed. And they had every right to protest, given that their tax dollars were transferred to a few of these banks. This is one of the inherent lunacies of Keynesian polices; the government sometimes transfers wealth from the poor and middle-income earners to the very rich and well-connected.

OWS created a clever slogan about the 99 per cent vs. the 1 per cent. It is clever because it is a mathematical given that there will always be a 99 per cent and a 1 per cent, regardless of how rich or poor a society is and how big the gap between rich and poor. There will *always* be a 1 per cent, so these protestors designed a way to stay permanently angry. They twisted their message from protesting banks for receiving tax dollars, to complaining about inequality and calling for "social justice" — presumably meaning a more equal distribution of wealth forced by the government. This is also known as socialism.

What I recall most vividly from these protests (and the curious copycat protests that occupied Canadian cities and parks despite the fact that Canada did not bail out any banks) is the students complaining about their massive student debt. Many photos circulating on the Internet featured people holding up signs showing the debt they had racked up earning their degrees, how they could not find work, and how long it would take them to pay back their loans.

While many of these folks were professional protestors (as pointed out by the good journalistic work of Ezra Levant and Sun News), many also had reasons for their grievances. These members of *generation screwed* had been sold a bill of goods. They had the expectation that a post-secondary education would put them on the path to a good middle class life. They were willing to become heavily indebted in order to achieve this goal. They understood that if they bit the bullet and paid inflated tuitions, it would pay dividends in their future. But graduating into a recession left them with few job prospects, dwindling career opportunities and expensive student debt. The cost of their education was greater than its value.

An economic bubble caused the soaring tuition fees for post-secondary education in the US (the government guaranteed loans, so banks were willing to lend more, so universities started to charge more, so banks started lending more, and so on). The result is that students began graduating with record debt; meanwhile, the prolonged financial recession meant that good job opportunities were rare. Debt became more daunting. This problem of personal consumer debt and student debt became a focus in the public discourse following the Occupy Wall Street movement. Many occupiers demanded amnesty for their student loans, and demanded that the government bail them out instead of bailing out the banks. The OWS movement oddly began to devolve into an incoherent ransom note that made personal demands of the government, including things like paying off people's student loans (in fact, they demanded *all* debt to be forgiven, including mortgages and credit card debt), ending free trade and imposing stiff tariffs on foreign products but also allowing open borders for immigration, spending $2 trillion on infrastructure and planting trees, ending fossil fuels, and imposing government health care.

Oh the irony. Occupy Wall Street began because people were furious that banks had received taxpayer bailouts. So their response: to demand their own bailout! OWS proved that they were no different from the people they were protesting. They were rent-seekers, driven by envy, not justice.

Student debt vs. Government debt

Despite its inevitable degeneration into some kind of anarchist, anti-capitalist commune, the original tenants of Occupy Wall Street — as with the Tea Party — had legitimate concerns about the unhealthy relationship between big business and big government. Many in *generation screwed* felt it was unfair that banks were bailed out after making poor and risky decisions about real estate speculation, while they were not bailed out for their poor and risky decisions to drive themselves into debt for post-secondary education.

Unlike government debt, your student debt will eventually be paid off. You will need to be disciplined, responsible, and learn how to save, but you will pay it off. Student debt can even be motivating. It makes you work hard and forces you to be ambitious in the early part of your career. If you believe in your future earning potential, and take on debt to put yourself in a better position to achieve success, it is worth it. It was always confusing to me, during the OWS era, to see people who had acquired three or four university degrees, accumulated hundreds of thousands of dollars in student debt, but could not find a job to pay back their loans. Why on earth would you allow yourself to go *that* far into debt? Why did you go back for the third or fourth degree? Bad decisions should not be rewarded, especially through public policy and taxpayer dollars. Debt should work to dissuade people from getting into these kinds of situations. It is shocking that a bank would continue to lend to such a person, but government guarantees made the banks forgo better judgment. As for the indebted, it is ultimately their responsibility to repay their debts.

At my school, the University of Alberta, a similar charade took place with the Student Union's "Wall of Debt." Students would write down the debt they owed on a piece of paper and tape it onto a wall. I remember watching a guy with a Gucci bag, wearing designer jeans and J Lindeberg sweatshirt write that he owed $125,000 in debt. $125k! Tuition at the time was less than $7,000 per year, and this guy did not look like he had been in school for 16 years, so my assumption was that he was using his student loans to finance a lifestyle, not just an education. This is no one's fault but his own.

Regardless of such outliers, the average Canadian student graduates with $14,453 in debt. This could be higher — our American neighbours typically graduate with double that, averaging $30,000 in student debt — but Canadian students work hard to fund their own education. Almost 60 per cent of students hold a job while in school, and the vast majority has a paying summer job. This work ethic helps prepare Canadian students for their career and savings. Speaking from personal experience, a $14,000 student loan can easily be paid off within a year or two if you are diligent. Financing big government activism and the welfare state, on the other hand, will be your burden over the course of your lifetime. *Generation screwed* is rightfully concerned about debt, but I suggest you focus on the debt that will deplete your career earnings, rather than the one that helps enable your career.

Compare your $14,453 in student debt with the structural debt built into the government that you will inherit. If you break down our national debt, every man, woman and child in Canada is on the hook for $17,553. On average, Canadians owe another $17,832. If you live in Ontario or Quebec, your per capita provincial government debt is much higher, at $21,019 and $23,426, respectively. Add to that debt burden an additional $82,563 in future debt or unfunded government liabilities. That's how much money will be necessary to pay all those baby boomers the lucrative retirement benefits like health care, pensions and elderly benefits that have been promised to them by politicians. So far, your government debt tally is $117,948. But we're not done yet. Given that not every Canadian is a taxpayer, and therefore does not carry the burden of government debt, your individual burden is likely much higher (assuming you are or will soon be a productive, taxpaying member of society). Every tax paying Canadian has a government debt burden of $243,476. [3] That is how much poorer you will be thanks to the lop-sided schemes of the welfare state.

Debt is a problem. But there are certainly some kinds of debt that are more problematic than others. Next time you hear someone complain about student debt and about unfairness in our system, you might want to direct their attention to the real debt burden.

Recession is the New Normal

The financial crisis and subsequent recession did not create *generation screwed,* but it certainly brought attention to the troubles created by taking on too much debt. And the recession is far more than just a bump in the road. While governments continue to vainly shower borrowed money to "stimulate" the economy, the economy refuses to recover. But what if I told you that the economy is not going to recover, and that the lowered economic output during the better part of the last decade is here to stay? More and more economic thinkers are coming to this rather frightening conclusion.

We know that many of our problems stem from the fact that politicians and baby boomers had unrealistic and unfounded expectations about population growth. In assuming the same levels

---

[3] Figures from the Fraser Institute's Canadian Government Debt 2014: A guide to the Indebtedness of Canada and the Provinces, April 2014

of constant growth, politicians and bureaucrats imagined a way to fund the system that might be sustainable. Unfortunately, the very basis of their assumption was wrong, hence why you are *generation screwed*. The same can be said for the economy as a whole. It isn't growing like it is supposed to. The idea of never-ending economic growth that allowed governments to grow beyond their affordability, also contributes to the reason you will be poorer than your parents.

Tyler Cowen, economics professor at George Mason University, wrote about this phenomenon in his eBook, *The Great Stagnation*. The book argues that all the "low-hanging fruit" in the economy has been picked and eaten, and any future growth will be much more difficult and labour-intensive to achieve. Gone are the days when we could just assume five per cent economic growth each year. In fact, we are lucky if the economy grows at all. In many sectors, it is actually contracting. Dr. Cowen explains that our civilization and economy have benefited from such low-hanging fruit as free land (or conquered land), immigrant labour and powerful new technologies. These benefits started to diminish over the last 40 years, and so too did real growth and development. We are so used to endless growth that we tried to cheat, using government intervention to cover the fact that our economy is actually stagnant. This is the end of growth.

This might seem counter-intuitive, given the proliferation of technologies and the ways we communicate over the past decade. We have incredibly powerful — and incredibly cool — handheld computers; more people than ever have lifestyles that include riches like education, state-of-the-art health care facilities, and world travel, things that were reserved for the rich and well-connected only decades ago. But this is not real growth, certainly not in economic terms.

Speaking at the University of Toronto in 2012, Dr. Cowen explained his thesis through a simple story. His grandmother, born in 1905, experienced tremendous growth and real change during her lifetime, from the widespread adoption of electricity and indoor plumbing to antibiotics and penicillin. She witnessed the invention of automobiles and then planes and helicopters, which changed the concept of travel and the movement of goods. Radio and then television changed the way information was communicated and shared. And households were transformed with such timesaving inventions as the refrigerator, vacuum cleaners, microwave ovens, washers and dryers, irons, toasters, coffee makers, and electric sewing machines. These inventions played a role in the women's liberation movement, by allowing women to spend less time at home and more time in the public realm and the workforce. This truly was an extraordinary time to be alive, and grandmother Cowen witnessed the world change in such a significant way.

By contrast, Tyler Cowen was born in 1962. He posits that the same kind of changes will not occur in his lifetime, and that the world has not achieved the same growth and improvements. Sure, smart phones are fun and helpful, and our purchasing power has grown, allowing us to buy more things, but this is not the same as the growth of his grandmother's time. American income numbers reflect this theory. Between 1947 and 1973, inflation-adjusted median income in the US more than doubled. From 1973 to 2004, median incomes only grew by 22 per cent and since 2004 they have actually declined. If income levels had continued to grow at their pre-1973 rate, the median income in the US would be $90,000, instead of its current range of around $50,000.

There are no major technological breakthroughs on the horizon. And growth will not come easily. Dr. Cowen sees science as a major part of the solution, and calls for more scientists and entrepreneurs to be promoted through the education system. We need more scientists, more entrepreneurs and fewer bureaucrats. Until we can spur real economic growth again, the major problem we face will be learning to live within our means. Learning to live with less. *Generation screwed* will face the threat of living with a lot less. You will encounter higher taxes, higher premiums and higher prices, alongside lower incomes, lower growth and lower expectations.

PART III

THE NEW PLAGUE

Our economy is sick. We have been hesitant to give the patient the medicine it needs because that medicine is a tough pill to swallow. It requires short-term pain, in exchange for better health in the long run. The antidote for the sickness of big government and the welfare state will cause side effects, including many individuals losing the entitlements they believe they deserve. Many do deserve them. Many have paid into the system over a lifetime.

The problem is that they were paying into a Ponzi scheme. Fraudsters, dressed up as politicians and bureaucrats, have designed a system that benefits some (older generations and baby boomers) at the expense of others (*generation screwed*). The sickness is a society that doesn't pay its bills. A society that uses debt to live above its means and mortgages the future to pay for it all. As this sickness spreads, it will mean more borrowing and more debt until, eventually, the system collapses.

We can postpone the impact of the illness. But eventually it will spread. It will turn into a plague.

The solutions usually prescribed by politicians to overcome *generation screwed's* problems, for instance premium adjustments and tax hikes, are the equivalent of giving ibuprofen to a patient suffering from brain cancer. Yes, Advil may help with the headaches. But headaches are a symptom of the tumour, and taking Advil does not typically cure tumours. When dealing with cancer, you need to go to the source. You need to remove the tumour.

Big government and the welfare state are past the point of tinkering to prolong the life of the system for a few extra years. Big government is a cancer on our economy and our society, and this plague will only spread faster and faster over the coming decades. The problem is not just about one unsustainable program. There are dozens of them, all underwritten by taxpayers. And all a particularly bad deal for young and future taxpayers.

You will have to deal with the consequences of big government and figure out how to fix some of the most challenging problems ever encountered. These problems include:

- Annual deficits without concern for balancing the budget

- Chronic and institutional overspending

- Accumulated debt piling up year after year

- Annual interest payments eating up more of the budget

- Entitlement programs that are crumbling at the foundation and being mended temporarily with Band-Aid solutions

- More and more unaffordable big promises from politicians

- Unfunded liabilities in such pension schemes as the CPP, OAS and GIS

- Medicare and the looming cost proliferation as baby boomers retire and live longer than ever.

- Government failing at its core functions, resulting in persistent under-funding of infrastructure

- Canadian government programs and special tax breaks that cost taxpayers $45,000 a year per senior

- An anemic economy producing stagnant wages

But as long as baby boomers are running the country — they are now, and will be for another decade or two — the response will be more of the same. They will hike contributions for new and young taxpayers. They will continue to pile on public debt for future generations of taxpayers to deal with. They will simply kick the can farther and farther down the road, until it is someone else's problem to deal with. *Your problem.* They will shirk responsibility and put their generation ahead of *generation screwed.* That is why it is up to you and your peers to tackle these problems and demand a better deal. Otherwise, baby boomer politicians will simply continue to screw you over.

ABOVE THE SURFACE

"A promise made is a debt unpaid."

— Robert Service, Canadian Poet

This book aims to highlight the impending economic and political crises of our time. To better understand *how* this is going to happen, this section examines the actual structural problems here in Canada, at all levels of government. As I mentioned earlier, the problem for *generation screwed* can be imagined as an iceberg that we are sailing towards. The tip of the iceberg is above the surface, and can be clearly seen with the naked eye. Similarly, we can point to these issues now and flag them as troublesome. These are the obvious problems that are often discussed by academics, think tanks, advocacy groups, journalists and politicians across the country. Most reasonable folks agree that these problems exist and ought to be dealt with. Annual deficits, accumulating debt, interest on the debt, government spending, taxes and the budgeting process. These are problems that are hidden in plain sight.

Hidden under the water is the rest of the iceberg. We will get to these problems in the next section — the problems that are being kicked down the road, the ones that will explode in your lifetime but the ones that we don't often hear about because they are hidden beneath the surface.

As for today's problems, they will only worsen if they are not addressed. If they continue to be ignored, permitted, excused or met with apathy, as is increasingly the case, they will simply turn into the much larger problems of tomorrow.

DEFICITS & DEBT

"I sincerely believe, with you, that banking establishments are more dangerous than standing armies; and that the principle of spending money to be paid by posterity, under the name of funding, is but swindling futurity on a large scale."

— Thomas Jefferson, in a letter to John Taylor, 1816

Deficits and debt are the consequences of big government. Governments of all stripes overspend. They have expanded to the point where, despite record high revenues, there is not enough money in the coffers to cover the costs of all those big promises. Tax hikes are deeply unpopular, so governments opt to borrow instead. These are symptoms of the disease, and the result of a government that does not live within its means. This chapter focuses on how governments raise money, how they spend it, and how their big borrowing schemes are nothing but a tax on the future.

Much like an individual, household or business, the government has income and it has expenses. Unlike an individual, a household or business, the government can easily ignore the numbers on its budget, or change them when needed. Remember, politicians get to write and re-write the rules whenever necessary. Governments do not have their own money; everything they have comes from the power of taxation, the power to take money from taxpayers. This income, known as government revenue, is collected through taxes, fees and other funds raised from government assets and state-owned enterprises. Revenues are based on taxation levels and the types of taxes imposed, which of course the government can change at any time, often with just the stroke of a pen.

Government expenditures are all the money that governments spend. Governments overextend themselves trying to fulfill all those big promises and pay the big salaries for all those government employees, not to mention all their other core functions like building critical infrastructure and administering our justice system. When you take all the money government collects through taxes and other revenues, and subtract all the money the government doles out in program spending, bribes, and social entitlements, we get either a budget deficit or surplus.

If it is a positive number, we call it a surplus. These are incredibly rare. In fact, in the 2009-10 fiscal year, no government in Canada had a surplus. All ten provinces and the feds spent more money than they brought in. The next year, only Newfoundland and Labrador and Nova Scotia had surpluses, and in 2013-14, only Saskatchewan managed to balance its books. Budget surpluses are not necessarily good for taxpayers. Yes, it means that governments did not overspend from its own estimates. But it doesn't mean good governance, per se. A budget surplus simply means the government collected *too much* revenues and taxes, which diminishes economic output in the economy. Governments should respond to surpluses by either cutting taxes to keep more productive capital in the market instead of sitting in government coffers, or, if the government has debt, by allocating the surplus towards paying down government debt. Too often, neither of these options is followed, and politicians just find some new pet project to throw money at.

The vast majority of time, however, governments spend more than they collect, leaving a negative figure known as a budget deficit. This is the norm in Canada. Every province and the feds regularly run deficits most years. This is both because they can and because they just cannot discipline themselves to balance the books. More often than not, deficits are structural or operating deficits. This simply means that the problem is not a one-time imbalance due to an unforeseen event like a big government bailout or lost revenues from a large company moving away. These are deficits that come year after year because the government's operating expenses exceed its revenues. Instead of raising taxes to cover the costs, or even better, cutting spending so that it balances revenues, politicians take the easy way out, and borrow the difference by running a deficit.

Of course, an individual, household or business could not get away with this. If you spent more money than you made each and every month, you would have to borrow. Over time, you could max out your credit card, take bank loans, mortgage any property you may own, and borrow from family members or friends. You could resort to predatory lenders, like pawn shops, credit shops or cash advances. Eventually and inevitably, you would get cut off. Banks would deny you any more loans. You'd start receiving phone calls and collectors would start threatening you or taking your stuff. They would talk to your bank, which would eventually freeze your accounts and start to dock your pay. You would have no choice but to pay back your loans or file for bankruptcy.

But for governments and politicians, the same consequences do not exist. (Or at least our elected politicians don't think these consequences exist.) At the end of the year, that imbalance — the deficit — merely gets added to the total outstanding debt. In a politician's mind, it gets banished to Siberia never to be heard from again. So year after year after year, irresponsible politicians toss more and more onto our debt and dig us deeper and deeper in the hole, hoping no one will notice. And most people don't. The annual deficit shortfall quietly gets added to the cumulative amount owed, the debt. And this debt mounts bigger and bigger, year after year.

As mentioned, if a government runs a budget surplus, it could put those surplus funds towards the debt, but in practice, this rarely occurs. Ontario ran surplus budgets from 2005 to 2008, collecting over $3 billion more in taxes than was spent by government, and yet, over that same period, Ontario's debt grew by just shy of $4 billion. How is this possible? It is possible because no one is paying attention and politicians should not be trusted! Sneaky governments have moved to an "accrual" accounting system, which means they separate their budget into two separate documents, and have a "cash" budget to show flows in and out in the year, and a "secondary" budget for long-term building projects that get expensed over the life of the project.

So even if it looks like a balanced budget, as we've seen recently in Alberta, which recently moved to this method of accounting — or some bastardized version of it — politicians are still burying you with debt because they are building infrastructure and not counting it as an annual expenditure in the budget. There is nothing wrong with building infrastructure. In fact, it is one of the few areas where a good free market alternative has not really emerged. The problem is that governments collect billions of dollars in taxes ostensibly for infrastructure without investing them appropriately. Gasoline taxes and driver fees were brought in specifically for bridge, tunnel and roadway building and maintenance. Instead, these tax revenues go to fund the welfare state, and infrastructure is either neglected or financed through more debt, and hidden out of sight in a secret secondary budget that never gets discussed.

Many politicians have convinced themselves that borrowing and accumulating debt is fine, and there are no consequences. They are convinced that they can borrow like there is no tomorrow. And debt apologists — like John Maynard Keynes and Keynesian economists discussed in Part One — tell politicians that debt is totally fine.

These apologists perpetuate the idea that government debt is just a fact of life in modern government, and thereby give politicians the opportunity to do and spend however they please. There are no parameters around politicians and their outrageous spending habits. They can dream up whatever crazy idea imaginable and then use your money to fail miserably trying to implement it. Or they can win elections by forever promising more money to special interest groups and bribing people with their own money. Money, of course, they do not have. Money they are borrowing.

And the reason pro-debt economists say it's okay to borrow? Because governments have the power of taxation. They get to use all the money in the economy — all of the money you earn, and all the money I earn, and all the money brought in by every business and government in the country — as collateral. Debt is measured in a ratio with the GDP, the gross domestic product (or the total income a the country), not just of government, but also of the entire economy (including the government).

$$GDP = C + G + I + NX$$

C = Private Consumption & Consumer Spending
G = Sum of all Government Spending
I = Businesses Capital Spending
NX = Net Exports (Exports - Imports)

Debt apologists say the only number that really matters is the debt-to-GDP ratio because it compares debt to the entire size of the economy. Why does this number matter? It suggests that, if they really needed to, the government could simply *take* all the money from the economy it wants. Government could impose brazen new taxes to take hundreds of billions of dollars from its people in order pay back government debts. The debt-to-GDP comparison merely shows the damage that would be done, should the government ever be put in a position where it *had* to pay its debt, the way you or I do.

It is important to note that indebted governments are *not* the ones that decide when they must pay back those debts. It is up to bond lenders, who at any time could start to demand the money be paid back by no longer buying new government bonds. What if something changes and we could no longer access more credit? What if we actually had to repay the debt now? We would be in big trouble. Just take a look at what the debt apologists think is an acceptable debt-to-GDP level. Combined debt across federal and provincial governments in Canada is currently around $1.2 trillion; Canada's total GDP is around $1.8 trillion, so our debt-to-GDP ratio is currently around 66 per cent!

There are at least two very misleading aspects of this measure. First, GDP measures the entire economy, *including government spending*. How can you measure growth or the value in the economy when you are including the artificial spending growth within the government sector, including a significant portion of borrowed funds? It is misleading to think of government spending within GDP, and then also compare the GDP as a ratio to government spending and debt.

The second problem is that the debt-to-GDP measurement is based on our net debt, or total bonded debt minus all government assets. But many assets, hydro infrastructure for instance, are not easily converted into cash. Could the government sell a subway station or school to pay down debt? Highly unlikely. But these are included and offset when we talk about net debt.

To make matters even worse, net debt is also offset by supposed "surpluses" built up in public pension funds. Imagine a pension fund that has a balance of $100 million, with annual payouts of $50 million and annual revenue of $40 million. The government considers this $100 million an asset, even though the money is spoken for, and the fund is decreasing at a rate of ten per cent each year. As was recently pointed out in a report by the IMF, this is also misleading. Just because the balance of a pension fund is positive doesn't mean there is actually a surplus. The money in those funds has already been accounted for. It has already been promised away. In fact, the promised funds outweigh the current balance; so those "surpluses" are actually just future debt, or unfunded liabilities.

Using pension balances as an asset to offset the total debt owed is completely misleading. It is just another sneaky way politicians and bureaucrats are hiding the truth and just how bad things really are.
When the IMF dissected Canada's books, they found the real debt-to-GDP ratio to be 87 per cent. This is the 13th highest among the advanced Western economies. Are you worried yet?

Provinces are guilty of this practice of hiding the real debt-to-GDP ratio as well. Quebec is in the worst shape in the county, with a provincial ratio of 51 per cent. Ontario is not far behind at 40 per cent. When you combine provincial and federal debt burdens, the ratio rises to 87 per cent for Quebec and 76 per cent in Ontario. According to the IMF definitions, once you account for the practice of offsetting debt with unusable assets, the figure rises by about 20 per cent above reported levels. Municipal debt is also excluded from the way provincial governments record net debt. So, despite what politicians say, the real debt in Ontario and Quebec are already more than 100 per cent of the economy, with the definition of the economy including government spending. If you shed away government spending, and simply look at the private economy, the figure becomes even more lopsided. Our debt in Canada's two largest provinces is significantly more than all the assets in the economy. This is a real cause for concern.

And yet, some economists and finance bureaucrats maintain that everything is just fine and dandy in Canadian government finances. It is difficult to even imagine what would be left of the economy once the government stripped its citizens of enough to pay off the debt.

The idea of a government running out of money isn't just something that happens in far-away places like Greece or Venezuela. It happened to both the Feds and the governments of Saskatchewan and Ontario in the 1990s. Ontario NDP Premier Bob Rae must have been shocked to be told by bureaucrats that they'd literally run out of money, and couldn't borrow any more. After trying, and failing, to spend his way out of an economic downturn in the 1991-92 budget, Bob Rae was forced to use the subsequent three budgets to introduce unpopular tax hikes and even less popular spending cuts, including wage cuts to his union base.

Debt by Government in Canada

	Debt		Debt
BC	$63,053,000,000	NB	$11,811,000,000
AB	$10,764,000,000	NS	$14,645,000,000
SK	$4,594,000,000	PE	$2,006,000,000
MN	$31,367,000,000	NL	$9,344,000,000
ON	$274,624,000,000	FED	$613,000,000,000
QC	$201,574,000,000	TOTAL	$1,236,782,000,000

Source: Canadian Taxpayers Federation. Provincial and Federal Debt Clocks. October 2014

It's possible for governments to roll up massive amounts of debt because they have far more power and leverage than citizens. But it is untrue that debt comes without consequences. Debt apologists may be correct in saying that, yes, technically, governments have the power to impose 100 per cent taxation and take all the money they need from the economy to pay back their debts. But short of that hypothetical, even the least bad result of debt is pretty terrible. The price of debt is high, and extends beyond just the cost of interest payments on the debt.

Bond, Government Bond

Governments borrow through bond markets, where debt is issued and sold though auctions. Bonds are fixed financial assets sold on an exchange market where buyers are promised specified interest, yields and a repayment schedule from the issuer. They are essentially IOUs. Governments issue bonds that are to be repaid in 2, 5, or 10-year periods, and traders buy them, thereby giving governments the money they need in the short-term. Bond prices are issued based largely on interest rates and on the ability of the issuer to meet its payment obligations, based on assessments by credit rating agencies. Governments are considered very safe issuers; they are unlikely to default because they have that power of taxation. Bond prices can also be based on other factors, like political stability, taxation rates, government spending, liabilities and economic performance. Bonds expire after their set maturity date, so even if the government runs a miraculous surplus, it still needs to frequently issue new bonds to pay for old debt. Governments are in a constant cycle of issuing new debt and constantly looking for new borrowers. They are using one credit card to pay the interest on the other. They are taking out mortgages to pay down lines of credit, and lines of credit to pay back older mortgages. And the interest payment on all these debts is substantial.

There are also unintended consequences to big government borrowing. Since government bonds are considered safer than corporate bonds, these are the first choice of lenders and investors. Instead of investing in the private sector, investors tie up trillions of capital in buying government debt. They make safe investments in the government sector, instead of investing in innovation, creativity and progress. This money would be much better spent invested and lent to start-ups and entrepreneurs in the wealth-producing sectors of the economy, rather than wasted away by politicians on pet projects and the bloated bureaucracy. Government bonds take away other opportunities for capital to be utilized in research and development, and spur real growth. This is the opportunity cost of capital investments in government debt.

The other major consequence of debt is the interest we pay in servicing the debt. In both Ontario and Quebec, taxpayers fork over about $11 billion per year just to cover the interest payments. That is nine per cent and 12 per cent, respectively, of all expenditures in those provinces. And the federal debt eats up 13 per cent of its entire budget. This is a substantial amount of money to pay for nothing: for the past mistakes of past governments, enabled by past voters, carried out by past politicians. Thanks to compound interest, or the convoluted way interest is calculated, we actually pay interest on the interest of our debt.

Interest rates are very low at the moment, so debt is cheap. Central bankers have used monetary policies to keep these rates artificially low in order to create an incentive to borrow; the justification being that this cash injection will "jump start" the economy. Since debt is cheap, both consumers and politicians are given more opportunities to borrow.

But this charade cannot go on forever. Interest rates will eventually go back up, and when they do, the cost of serving our government debt will go through the roof. A rise in interest rates will cause the cost of our debt to grow exponentially. At the height of Canada's debt problems of the early 1990s, interest on government debt comprised 36 per cent of all government spending. That is largely because interest rates were higher in the 90s, whereas today, they are at an all-time low.

Historic Interest Rate for Government of Canada Debt

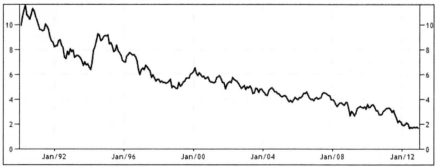

Source: Government of Ontario, Ministry of Finance.

Interest rates manipulated by central bankers are just another

Keynesian tool to stimulate growth. And just like stimulus spending, the long-term consequences of manipulating interest rates are far worse, and far outweigh any benefit from the artificial, short-term growth. Interest rates used to be set and determined by individual banks, and the rate would represent how much reserve funds the bank held, as well as the trustworthiness of the borrower. In good economic times, people would have healthy surpluses and growing savings accounts; banks therefore had more money to lend and could offer lower interest rates. When times were bad, there were fewer people saving and less money to lend out; consequently, interest rates were higher to discourage non-essential borrowing. Interest rates were a market signal, and would communicate to potential borrowers the cost of debt based on the supply of money held by lenders.

Today, things are different. Central bankers use monetary policies like quantitative easing to artificially lower interest rates as part of their overall policy to stimulate fake demand in the economy. Interest rates are used to manipulate behaviour and encourage more borrowing and debt.

The reason our interest rates are at a 20-year low is to create incentives for people to take on more debt so it will look like the economy is recovering and growing. This misguided Keynesian policy is a dangerous game for central bankers to play; it makes debt cheap, creating false incentives for people to buy houses and take loans and make bad economic decisions. Cheap debt makes people bid up on prices and creates a mirage of growth, when really it is just a bidding war caused by surplus cash. And as economic history tells us about these economic bubbles — whether it be in the housing market, student loans, tulips in the 16th century or the dot-coms in the late 1990s — they eventually pop, and a lot of people lose a lot of money.

Eventually our interest rates will go back up. Everyone knows this.

They cannot stay artificially low forever, and economists and financial experts constantly speculate about when this will happen. This is the ticking time bomb for our large government debt. Once interest rates increase, our debt will get much, much, much more expensive to service. Because government bonds are constantly reissued, new bonds will carry higher costs. More and more of government's revenues will be eaten up by interest payments. Less and less of what governments collect will be available for social programs as they scramble to keep the bond lenders at bay. Canada's top tax expert, Professor Jack Mintz of the Calgary School of Public Policy, calculates that for every point the interest rate increases, Ontario's annual interest payments will grow by $3 billion.

The long-term consequences of debt are even more depressing. Today's debt becomes tomorrow's taxes. Aside from throwing away tens of billions in annual interest payments to service this debt each and every year, eventually our debts will be called in. Eventually we will have to pay it all back to the bond lenders. And when we do, it will compromise our entire society. All those promises made by all of the politicians will become impossible. It will mean higher taxes and reduced services; a reduction in core and front-line services such as health care, education and social welfare, not to mention government pensions. Our tax dollars simply will not go as far as we are used to, and reluctantly, our politicians will be forced to raise taxes. With more taxes and less money in our pockets, plus less of our tax money going to government services, we can expect a real drop in our standard of living.

Here is the unpleasant truth: you will be poorer than your parents, in both relative and real terms. This is the long-term consequence of bad government decisions like debt.

Debt and the cost of borrowing is the real threat to government services. Despite what you may have heard, it is not scary conservative politicians that may cut government services to balance the budget. We should actually mistrust the irresponsible politicians who ignore balancing the budget and opt to borrow instead. They are ignoring the long-term problems in favour of short-term ease. The unintended consequences of our democracy, where politicians bribe voters with borrowed money, is a lifetime of debt dropped on the shoulders of *generation screwed.*

Greece's Debt Crisis - What happened?

Big bonuses, lucrative pensions and early retirement for government employees. Out of control spending, huge deficits, and mounting public debt. Sound familiar? This is what led to the debt crisis in Greece. Greece had countless interventionist policies that manipulated prices and wages in the economy, from a mandatory 14-month salary compensation package, to mass bailouts and corporate welfare, to powerful labour unions that prevented privatization or private competition in much of the economy. In late 2009, the major credit rating agencies all began to downgrade Greece's credit, thereby driving up the cost of debt and limiting Greece's ability to borrow. After being cut off from most of the bond market — the equivalent of cutting up the high interest credit cards of a shopping addict — Greece could no longer afford to pay its bills and began requesting international bailouts to cover the government's everyday housekeeping expenses, such as paying salaries and pension obligations. Eventually, the European Union and the IMF grudgingly bailed Greece out, on the condition that it would drastically reduce spending and work to balance its budget. These "austerity measures" led to riots and chaos in the streets of Athens and across the country. It was the credit rating downgrades, reacting to Greece's debt burden that sparked the beginning of the European Debt Crisis.

SPENDING & BUDGETING

"For years, governments have been promising more than they can deliver, and delivering more than they can afford."

— Former Prime Minister Paul Martin

"We don't have a trillion-dollar debt because we haven't taxed enough; we have a trillion-dollar debt because we spend too much."

— Former US President Ronald Reagan

Debt eventually catches up to you. For individuals, this happens faster than it does for governments. But that doesn't mean governments are exempt from the consequences of debt. Eventually, indebted governments will face the same reality as indebted individuals; they will be forced to shape up and address their financial problems. Whether there is a swing in public opinion due to education or advocacy about debt, or whether it is because of rising interest rates and credit downgrades, sooner or later our politicians will be forced to find a path to a balanced budget and debt repayment. In the last chapter, I explained how borrowing has become the favoured option for politicians, because it gives the illusion of balancing the public chequebooks. But when borrowing is no longer an option, politicians will be left with only two options: cut spending or raise taxes. That is, either adjust the spending side of the ledger or the revenue side. This chapter explores these options and provides a real life example of a government that was forced into such reforms.

Love thy Country, Not thy Government

There is a movement stemming from the intellectual left in Canada that has been calling for higher taxes. The Canadian Centre for Policy Alternatives, a far-left think tank, has been running a campaign called "I HEART TAXES" — trying to convince people that it is patriotic to pay taxes. They believe we ought to *want* to pay them. Good luck with that! Something is not patriotic if it is coercive. Loving your country is not the same thing as loving its government. Nobody "loves" having money taken away from them. Especially when it goes to wasteful spending, programs we disagree with and even fraud. Our money is just that, ours. Our salaries do not belong to the government; our money belongs to us. And individual Canadians know much better than a far off central government about our own needs, wants and desires.

You can spend your money better than a government. You can allocate it both more efficiently and in a way more personally beneficial. So do not be fooled into thinking that the government deserves your money or that it is patriotic to be fleeced by them.

Governments are not good stewards of our tax dollars. Money is constantly wasted. It is eaten up by administrative costs, pet projects and risky experiments. It is redistributed from younger generations to older ones, and sometimes, from the poor to the wealthy.

Operating deficits are not generally fixed through tax hikes. Raising taxes merely enables more big government. By paying higher taxes, we are permitting government growth. We are saying: "it's fine, keep growing." But if you raise taxes to cover the spending growth in government, and do nothing to cap that growth, the new taxes will quickly fall short once again. You will continually be forced to hike taxes to cover the continual growth in government spending. It will only stop when the focus is switched to the other side of the ledger, the spending side. And despite the bizarre campaigns on the left to promote higher taxes, new taxes will always be deeply unpopular with the people. No politician wants to be the sales person of constant tax hikes.

It is only through spending cuts and restraints that a government can get its books back in order. Sure, it can hike taxes too, but spending restraints are the necessary tool to get out of the trap of perpetual budget deficits. According to economist Dr. Dan Mitchell of the Cato Institute, a libertarian think tank in Washington, DC, the golden rule for public finances is that government spending should never grow faster than growth in the economy.

Dan Mitchell's Golden Rule:

Government spending should never grow faster than growth in the economy.

This is a politically feasible reform, according to Mitchell, because Keynesians and social advocates will remain happy if government is still permitted to grow, but since it is growing slower than the economy, the government becomes relatively smaller, and therefore more affordable. This simple rule confronts the disease of big government. Instead of looking for a short-term solution to balance the budget for a year or two, it goes to the core of excessive government. The more restraints and limits on government, the better. And spending restraints have proven to be the most effective tool to slay deficits, reduce debt levels and tackle big government.

After all, Canada has been in this position before. In the early 1990s, Canada's federal government was met with a debt crisis similar to the early stages of what happened in Greece in 2008. The Liberal government was dealing with run-away spending, staggering debt and an overtaxed population. So there was only one thing left to do. Cut spending. And they did. They managed to avoid a debt crisis by following the Golden Rule. Between 1992 and 1997, the Chrétien Liberals managed to keep the average annual growth in federal spending to below one per cent. With 0.8 per cent growth during those years, significantly lower than GDP growth, the debt-to-GDP ratio fell by 9.4 per cent and deficit-to-GDP by 9.3 per cent. They fixed the problem by slowing the growth of spending.

The Chrétien-Martin reforms

As briefly discussed in Part Two, Canada's fiscal turnaround in the 1990s is a remarkable story. It is a case study worth examining, and not just for Canadians, but for anyone interested in fiscal reforms that made government responsible and work better.

In a 1994 bond auction selling Canadian debt, the auction reached its final 30 minutes without a single bid. No one wanted to buy Canadian debt. Canada had a very different fiscal reputation back then, and given our fiscal record and debt, we were not a good candidate to would-be lenders. It was too risky. No one wants to lend to a government that could potentially default. And our country's abhorrent fiscal recording was finally catching up to us.

Eventually, however, a buyer did come through and the federal government was able to raise the funds it desperately needed. But it also received a new credit downgrade, as Standard & Poor's downgraded Canadian foreign currency debt down from AAA. The Wall Street Journal famously called Canada "an honorary member of the Third World." This was incredibly embarrassing and a massive wakeup call for newly elected Liberal Prime Minister Jean Chrétien. Canada's dirty laundry was being aired for the world to see, and a generation of big government fuelled by debt was coming back to haunt us. The emperor had been exposed with no clothes. This was the moment when everyone realized just how bad the situation was, and by this point, a simple Band-Aid solution wouldn't help. Merely slowing the pace of spending growth was no longer an option. The Chrétien government had to take drastic measures to shrink the actual size of government and scale back some of the biggest promises made to the Canadian people.

> "I said to myself, I will do it. I might be Prime Minister for only one term, but I will do it."

> — Former Prime Minister Jean Chrétien

When Jean Chrétien and the Liberals were first elected in November 1993, they quickly recognized the dreadful state of the country's books. Progressive Conservatives under Brian Mulroney and Kim Campbell may have brought free trade agreements with the United States and sold off cumbersome state-owned enterprises, but their fiscal track record was abysmal. True, they inherited massively expanded federal programs and a federal government under Pierre Trudeau that had lost any shred of responsibility or fiscal prudence, but the Mulroney government did very little to scale back those programs or stop the fiscal bleeding, aside from imposing the hated GST.

In reaction to the apparent death of fiscal conservatism in the federal party, reactionary organizations began to grow. The new Reform Party — dedicated to lowering taxes and balancing the budget — surged during the 1993 election, winning 52 seats compared to only two PC seats. As the major national opposition party in Canada, Reform leader Preston Manning ran a "zero-in-three" campaign, demanding a balanced budget in three years. Grassroots citizen-led advocacy organizations such as the Canadian Taxpayers Federation and the National Citizens Coalition were formed and grew from the outrage and frustration with the way Canada was being managed. These groups tapped into a strong sentiment for reforms held by many Canadians, and successfully organized rallies, protests and town hall meetings to discuss much-needed fiscal reforms.

This created a perfect storm in Ottawa. With a vocal opposition party representing a broad populist movement, fervent advocacy organizations like the CTF playing a larger role than ever in the public policy debates, and the sheer embarrassment of the credit downgrades and unsuccessful bond auctions, change was inevitable. Chrétien's Liberals were backed into a corner; they were left with no choice. They had to rein in spending. And so they did. It was not easy, but they managed to manoeuvre their way through it. The result speaks for itself. These reforms put Canada in an excellent position to weather the storms of the late 2000s, and represent one of the greatest and most dramatic fiscal Cinderella stories in modern history.

How did they do it? What did they cut? How did they get away with it? This is what many historians, economists and financial journalists are now revisiting. Even with all the forces pushing the Liberals towards reform, the job of fixing our finances was still a challenge almost beyond belief. It is incredibly difficult — indeed, nearly impossible — to roll back a government program or entitlement. Citizens become very attached to the big promises made by politicians over the years. And in the case of the Liberals, their core belief as a party centered on a big, activist government. They are the party of big government, and they truly believe in it. They want the government to be a force for good in everyone's life. This very idea terrifies me. But to Liberals, this is the center of their worldview. This made scaling back big government all the more challenging.

Not only did the Chrétien Liberals have to convince the public at large and some political opponents, perhaps more challenging, they had to convince their party's rank and file. They had to convince *themselves*. Finance minister Paul Martin's father had been a Liberal cabinet minister and was one of the politicians who brought in one of Canada's biggest and most expensive promises: the single-payer government health care program, Medicare. Now, just a few decades later, Paul Martin Jr. was implementing massive cuts to this program. By fixing Canada's financial imbalance, however, Martin surely saved these programs from bankruptcy.

Federal Debt under each Prime Minister ($ billions)

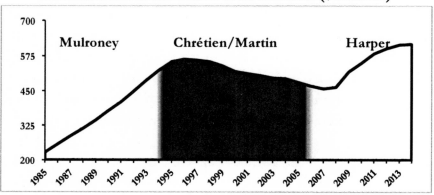

Source: Government of Canada. Archived Fiscal Reference Tables, Ministry of Finance.

Just one look at Canada's accumulated debt says it all. Spending was out of control; consecutive administrations allowed the government to grow without any concern for the future. This government growth was enabled by borrowing, and our debt began to soar.

At a 1994 cabinet meeting, Paul Martin announced that they would be implementing a full spending freeze. Every government department was responsible for cutting spending. When Martin announced this freeze, one cabinet minister put up his hand asking for an exception for a project. Chrétien said no. Another minister raised his hand to also ask for more funding. Chrétien apparently snapped and said that if anyone else asked for more money, their department would face a 20 per cent cut. The room went silent. He was serious. There was no room for negotiations. It had to be done.

The reforms started with fixing Employment Insurance entitlements and changing the formula to pay the unemployed. They then cut defence spending and chopped foreign aid. But that was not enough. The 1994 budget showed modest reforms, but Canada's deficit was still too high. Moody's Investors Services lowered its rating of Canada's credit, citing government debt as the reason for the downgrade.

Chrétien and Martin continued to cut spending in industry, transportation, business subsidies and transfer payments to the provinces, including health care transfers, all while only imposing modest tax increases. In the end, the tax hikes were trivial; they increased revenue as a share of GDP from 44.2 per cent to 44.5 per cent. It was not tax hikes that got Chrétien and the Liberals out of hot water. It was spending cuts. In fact, the ratio of spending cuts to tax hikes was seven-to-one. According to Chrétien, "there was more need on one side than the other." There was a fundamental consensus in Canada that we had a spending problem, not a revenue problem. And the government recognized that the problem couldn't simply be swept under the rug with new taxes. We could no longer ignore the unmanageable size of the government. So they did the right thing. They cut spending. The cuts ranged from five per cent to

65 per cent of each department's budget. And their ambitious cuts paid dividends.

Spending fell year after year, and throughout Chrétien's entire term as leader. In just five years, between 1992 and 1997, government spending relative to GDP fell by more than nine percentage points, from 53 per cent of GDP down to 44 per cent. Adjusted to exclude interest payments on the debt, program spending fell 12 per cent per cent between 1994 and 1998. And with that, the deficit was erased. They followed the Cato Institute's golden rule on government budgeting. They kept spending growth below GDP growth. By ensuring that the economy was grower faster than the government, everything fell into place and the budget was balanced.

The 1995 budget is considered by many to be the most fiscally responsible budget in modern Canadian history. Chrétien and Martin addressed the problem head on, and the result was the largest reduction of spending in Canada since the demobilization after the Second World War. With good spending policy came good tax policy. A smaller government meant more surpluses and more opportunities for tax reform. Federal income tax was lowered and tax brackets were fully indexed to inflation, another issue the CTF and then-federal director Walter Robinson had championed. Taxes everywhere were lowered, on both individuals and businesses. The federal corporate tax rate fell from 28 per cent in 2000 down to 21 per cent in 2004. This allowed the Harper administration to cut corporate taxes even further, down to 15 per cent in 2014 and 11 per cent for small businesses. In many ways, the fiscal discipline of Chrétien and Martin set the stage for the Stephen Harper government tax reforms, such as cuts to the GST and the creation of the Tax-Free Savings Account. Canada is easily considered the strongest fiscal performer in the G7. This is largely due to the leadership of Chrétien and Martin and their fiscal reforms.

The Chrétien government left Canada in a much better fiscal situation than the one they were handed. The reasons they embarked on this crusade were circumstantial, not ideological. Regardless, their service and legacy are worth celebrating. But they did not fix everything. They failed to create the permanent condition for fiscal responsibility. Yes, they managed to rein in spending, but there was no guarantee future governments would do the same. The very next government engaged in stimulus spending that resulted in a decade of borrowing and new record-high debt. Health care and elderly benefits continue to soar to new heights, and once again put Canada's public finances at risk of defaulting. Instead of permanently tackling big government and dependency on big government, they merely fixed the problem for the moment by trimming the fat. Their solution was designed to postpone the problem and not upset the baby boomers. It did not fix the problem for *generation screwed.*

This gives *generation screwed* an idea of what needs to be done, and what lies ahead. Instead of reducing spending on a conditional, short-term basis, new reforms should go to the heart of the welfare state. It's clear from this example in recent Canadian history that when the Liberals addressed spending, the deficit and debt problems receded. By confronting the disease of spending, the symptoms of deficits and debt disappeared. But the deeper problem of spending — driven by big promises and the welfare state — is the real disease. And it's still very much alive in Canadian governments.

PART IV

BELOW THE SURFACE

"There is only one difference between a bad economist a good one: the bad economist confines himself to the visible effect; the good economist takes into account both the effect that can be seen and those effects that must be foreseen."

— Frédéric Bastiat

As promised, this section looks beneath the surface and to the problems down the road. Big governments and big spending in Canada are clearly a big problem. The problem was addressed and reduced under the Liberal reforms of the 1990s, but the deeper problem has not been solved. In fact, several provincial governments, especially Ontario and Quebec, are back on the exact same path that the feds were on, with excessive spending growth that far outpaces growth in the economy. We still have unmanageable deficits and growing debt. But these issues are not the focus of this section.

There is a whole new set of issues that will be encountered in the coming decades. Big spending is only half of the equation; the costs of dependency on the welfare state, particularly the universal government programs utilized by the elderly and retired, have not been pre-paid and are not properly funded. These future spending obligations are the other half of the equation for *generation screwed*, and unfortunately, they are a much bigger half.

Some of the problems below the surface are associated with those above the surface. As our government spending increases, so too does the number of government employees promised gold-plated benefits and unaffordable pensions. Others are separate, but stem from the same belief: that there are no limits to the role of government and its ability to fix every problem known to man. Or the belief that the government can spend your money better than you can, and that you cannot be trusted to take care of yourself. This includes such components of the welfare state as government health care, employment insurance and retirement saving. If you thought the $1.2 *trillion* in outstanding government debt was jarring, you may want to pour yourself a stiff drink before reading the next paragraph.

Below the surface, all those welfare state promises of pensions, health care and endless social programs have an outstanding price tag of $2.9 trillion. When combined with the net outstanding combined debt in Canada, we are buried under a mountain of $4.1 trillion in debt. For reference, our entire economy, Canada's GDP, is $1.821 trillion. The market value of all officially recognized goods and services produced in Canada over the course of an entire year equates to about 40 per cent of our entire outstanding financial obligations. Yikes!

This section will examine the programs that hide below the surface, including the Canada Pension Plan (CPP), Old Age Security (OAS), the Guaranteed Income Supplement (GIS), Medicare and the cost of government bureaucracies. None of these programs have been properly funded to cover the coming costs. We do not have enough saved, nor do we bring in enough in current revenues to pay for these programs. Politicians made promises far bigger than what they could afford. And if these programs are not reformed, if their shortfalls are not addressed — by restructuring the programs and changing the expectations of citizens — Canada will return to its pre-1995 fiscal status, as an honorary member of the Third World.

PENSION ENVY

"Public pensions are squarely based on what has been called the eighth wonder of the world — compound interest. A growing nation is the greatest Ponzi game ever contrived."

— Paul Samuelson, Nobel prize winner in economics

Government-managed pension funds exist because politicians do not trust individual Canadians to save for their own retirement. They don't trust that you will actually put aside enough or invest your money properly. They worry that if left to your own devices, you will either not save enough, or that your investments will be too risky. The great irony of this is the resulting government pension schemes deliver some of the worst returns in the market for young people.

Imagine if you had a good summer job and worked incredibly hard to save $10,000; money that you wanted to invest for your future. What if you went into the bank and they offered a pooled savings option that would give you the same returns at the Canada Pension Plan. Would you take it? The contribution value-to-benefit ratio on the CPP for anyone born after 1980 is only 0.66. Based on the rate of return on Canada's forced pension scheme, the bank would only invest $6,600 of your money for you and it would take $3,400 as a service fee.

No one would ever willingly take this deal. Even in a sluggish economy, the typical 20-year return on the TSX ranges from 6.6 per cent to 10.8 per cent. Our forced pensions plan takes away 34 per cent of young Canadians' money away! This is a scam. Any investor that offered their clients this return on investment would be laughed at or thrown in jail. But this is the deal *generation screwed* is forced into, without any choice. Our government pension schemes are a spectacular rip off. This chapter will provide a history of government pension promises in Canada, namely, the CPP, OAS and GIS. It will discuss new problems on the horizon, and specifically, why these pension schemes are a very bad deal for *generation screwed.*

There is a reason pension reform has long been called the "third rail" of Canadian politics. Most consider it too controversial and divisive to address. Since politics is the art of the possible, and at the end of the day politicians simply want to get re-elected, there are some issues and policies that remain off-limits. Pension reform tops this list. But regardless of the political aversion to tackling tough issues, sooner or later, political leaders will have to face the facts: our government-managed pensions are not sustainable. They are also incredibly unfair and discriminate against young workers. Further tinkering is inevitable because there is not enough money to fund all the pension benefits that have been promised, and the upcoming retirement avalanche will make this trend even worse. Young workers are already contributing more money than ever into pension plans, and the promised returns continue to diminish.

Canada's government-managed pensions are not properly funded. Both the CPP and government sector pension funds are dealing with the same general problems, namely that not enough money has been allocated into these funds historically to match the benefits owed, markets have not performed as well as forecasted, there are not enough new workers entering the workforce to replace the retiring exodus and retirees are living and therefore collecting longer than ever. The CPP picture looks bad; most government sector pension funds look far worse.

This has lead to operating shortfalls and deficits that have then been covered up through increased contributions. But there are obvious problems with throwing more money at the problem to help older Canadians retire better, and this is emphasized with looking at the biggest problem with the funding model for pensions: that they are a *very* bad deal for young Canadians.

The pooled funding system means that people do not contribute to their own retirement savings, but instead, young people pay the bills for those currently collecting. This type of funding is known in the real world as a Ponzi scheme. The scheme requires constant growth, but because the baby boomer cohort is much larger than subsequent generations, as baby boomers retire early and live longer, younger workers are required to pay more into the system than those collecting ever dd. A smaller workforce means that younger workers are required to pay more and more to pick up the slack. For instance, over the past two decades, our CPP contributions have been hiked by over 200 per cent. In 1994, the combined employee and employer CPP taxes were $1,612, whereas in 2014, they typical Canadian contributed $4,852 into the CPP fund. We are paying way more into the fund, but our benefits have not increased. And we can expect this trajectory to continue as the nine million Canadians retire over the next two decades.

A Brief History of Retirement Benefits

Government pensions are another invention of the welfare state. Politicians decided that people were not saving enough money for their retirement. So the government solution was to take more money *away* from people and save it for them! Another perhaps well-intended policy that has made us poorer as a result. And more dependent on the government. The initial government retirement program in Canada was geared toward assisting low-income seniors and those living in poverty. Not everyone is appropriately prepared for old age, ailing health and a sudden inability to provide and care for oneself. And not everyone has a family who can help. So the government came swooping in with a program aimed to support these individuals. In the midst of the post-war boom that brought us the welfare state, the government designed a specific welfare program aimed at struggling seniors.

In 1952, they introduced a scheme called Old Age Security (OAS). This is often confused with Social Security — the US's version of our Canada Pension Plan (CPP). OAS is different. It is not a pooled savings account where people contribute directly to the fund; it is a straight-up welfare program. No one contributes or pays directly into OAS. It is entirely funded by taxpayers through the government's general revenue. Seniors become eligible for OAS when they turn 65. In 1952, the average life expectancy of a Canadian was 69. The scheme was designed to typically support a recipient for three or four years. Today, the typical Canadian lives to age 81. This means the typical OAS recipient will collect this supplement for 16 years — 400 per cent of the original expectation. As the welfare state expanded, politicians saw new opportunities to court older voters, and thereby expanded OAS to include more and more of the population. Today, the vast majority of seniors receive this benefit; it is no longer just a program for the needy. OAS does not provide a large amount of money per person, but because of the sheer number of those now collecting the benefit, it is a significant portion of our government's budget.

The scheme works like this: once a Canadian turns 65, they become eligible for OAS. No matter their retirement status, savings or wealth, every senior is eligible to receive the base amount of $563.74 per month. If the individual is still working and receives an annual salary or pension of over $71,592, the government "claws back" a portion of the OAS. Keep in mind that the average income-tax filer in Canada, according to Statistics Canada, earns $52,000. So even if a senior is earning well above the average Canadian income, they are still eligible to receive the full OAS welfare supplement from taxpayers. The claw-back is progressive, meaning the more a senior earns, the more that gets removed from their monthly cheque.

The OAS benefit is fully removed at an income level of — wait for it — $116,103. Seniors that are married also have the tax benefit of being able to file taxes as a household — a practice known as "income splitting." This means that a couple could earn a combined $140,000 annually and still qualify for the full OAS. That married couple can earn as much as $231,432 in annual household income before their OAS benefits are fully clawed back.

This means that wealthy seniors earning almost five times that of the average Canadian tax-filer will still receive OAS welfare from the taxpayer. This is the arbitrary line where government deems a senior to be rich enough to no longer need this help from the taxpayer. This unbelievable and ridiculous double standard has hard-working, younger and lower-income taxpayers shovelling cash to wealthy, retired seniors — some still earning enough to be in the top five per cent of all income earners in the country.

The OAS benefit, while overly generous especially to middle and high-income earners, was still not enough. Politicians saw another opportunity to make big promises, so they introduced the Guaranteed Income Supplement (GIS) to offer even more to retired seniors. GIS is part of the OAS program, and gives single seniors an additional payment — as much as $764.40 per month, or $1,070.60 per month to a married couple earning below the minimum income threshold. While OAS is handed out to the vast majority of Canadian seniors, GIS has also been expanded to include about one out of every three Canadian seniors.

These programs have evolved from their original purpose, and the benefits have drastically increased thanks to everything from inflation to growing political pressure. The OAS scheme is Canada's largest retirement plan. It is eating up a larger and larger portion of our federal taxes. In 2013, taxpayers shelled out $43.7 billion to the OAS program: $33.1 billion in OAS, $10.4 billion in GIS and $151 million in administration cost. That is about 17.5 per cent of all federal spending! For context, that is more than double the federal government's entire budget for national defence.

There are 5.3 million Canadians collecting OAS, and of those, 1.8 million also collect GIS. This is one of the fastest growing government expenses in Canada. By 2015-16, the amount spent on elderly benefits will rise to $46.1 billion, and is projected to reach $54.1 billion by 2018. When you consider that an additional nine million Canadians will retire over the next 20 years, you can start to imagine how spending on these retirement programs will soar through the roof. According to a recent actuary report (which shows the math and the projected cost of the program over the next 40 years), in 2050, around the time I may expect to be retired, this program is expected to cost Canadians $200 billion annually. That is about the same amount as the federal government's total revenue in

2012! You can only imagine how much the government would need to hike taxes in order to meet this very tall order. They would have to at least quadruple tax revenues.

Our pension worries don't end with the mission creep of OAS and GIS. Remember, the welfare state transformed the role of government; it is no longer just a social safety net for the poor and needy. It has morphed, and now assumes responsibility for providing welfare to all citizens, regardless of their wealth. As such, just a decade after creating OAS, the government decided that *all* Canadians could benefit from government-mandated retirement savings. Forced savings into personal accounts was not good enough; politicians wanted the government to have more control, so they decided to create a forced pension scheme in which all funds are pooled together into a government-managed social insurance fund.

The Canada Pension Plan (CPP) was introduced in the mid-1960s under Liberal Prime Minister Lester B. Pearson. This was around the time the first baby boomers were entering the workforce, and the CPP required all workers to contribute 1.8 per cent of their income. Upon retirement, everyone who paid into CPP would begin to receive monthly cheques from the government. Not enough to live on, but a nice supplement to make people feel taken care of. And just as the OAS and GIS morphed from helping the least well-off into doling out funds to over five million Canadians, CPP goes to everyone who has contributed. And because contributions are mandatory for all working Canadians, CPP benefits are doled out even to millionaires and billionaires! This is another very costly promise by the government. Such a big promise, in fact, that one of the largest public policy debates (some say crisis) of the 1990s surrounded the very sustainability of the CPP fund. In December 1993, an actuary report found that based on projections, the fund would be bankrupt by 2015. Big reforms were needed, and politicians were forced to reconcile their big promises.

In 1997, changes were introduced, and resulted in a very bad deal for anyone born after 1975. Annual contributions to CPP were hiked from six per cent up to 9.9 per cent, shared equally by the employee and employer. In 1994, the typical Canadian worker earning an average income contributed $806 to the CPP annually; by 2004 that number had jumped to $1,832. In 2014, the typical Canadian worker contributed $2,464. We contribute 201 per cent more than workers just two decades ago.

CPP Payroll Tax Bill per Canadian Worker

Source: Nick Bergamini, Canadian Taxpayers Federation. New Year Tax Changes Report, 2014. Based on CRA Payroll Tax Rates.

Since the benefit rates are set by the government, rather than based on what an individual has contributed over the years, younger workers today pay more into the CPP fund than any other generation. This does not mean that younger workers will receive more in benefits. The opposite is true. The first cohort to collect CPP benefits were paid out 17 times what they paid in, whereas anyone born after 1975 will be lucky to receive two-thirds of what they have paid into CPP over a lifetime. Talk about a scam.

If you were born in 1985, you can expect your CPP contributions over your entire career to reach a value of $1.4 million, based on the amount you and your employer contribute, the CPPs rate of return and inflation. But, you will only ever collect a maximum benefit of about $900,000. A typical Canadian born in 1990 will have a contribution value of about $1.6 million, but only collect a maximum of little over $1 million. And those born in 1995 will have a CPP contribute value of $1.85 million, but only receive a maximum benefit of $1.2 million. This is because the CPP fund skims off your returns to pay out to today's recipients and fill any funding shortfalls. Can you imagine a bank doing that? Taking away the interest from your savings account to pay someone else's credit card bills? The government does this on a much larger scale, and behind closed doors. And only the government can force you into a retirement plan where you will lose $550,000 over your lifetime.

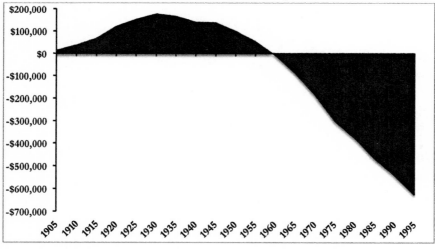

Return on Government Pension by Year of Birth

CPP return compared to expected value assuming constant growth. Credit Michael James.

Unlike a normal savings account where you can track and monitor your money, the CPP was designed as a "pay-as-you-go" scheme. Your CPP taxes are pooled together with all other CPP contributions from across the country, and paid out to current retirees as needed. At any given time, there is only enough in the fund to meet obligations for a few years, although the 1997 reforms made the CPP significantly more actuarially sound. Still however, the CPP is not fully funded for its future payment obligations. It manages to stay afloat because of current contributions, constant premium hikes and by deferring benefits for younger Canadians. If young Canadians stopped contributing to the fund, choosing instead to save for their own retirement, the CPP would go bankrupt. That is why you do not have a choice. The government has taken that choice away from you.

In 2012, the federal government again made modest changes to the OAS and GIS, moving the age of eligibility from 65 to 67, starting in 2023, or for folks born after 1957. They also started bribing people to defer collecting CPP until after age 70, offering a 30 per cent increase in benefits. This kind of tinkering can help prolong the collapse of these funds, but it certainly does not fix the problem. After the 1997 and 2012 reforms, the government now actually boasts that the CPP fund is 20 per cent funded and that it will be sustainable for the next 75 years. After that? Well, that's a problem for future taxpayers and future generations.

Pension Ponzi

In the 2012 Republican primaries, Presidential candidate and Texas Governor Rick Perry made a gaffe so large that it contributed to the end of his shot at the White House. In a heated exchange on Social Security (America's CPP), Perry called the plan a "Ponzi scheme." Many share this view, mostly because it is absolutely true by its very definition. But this is a very sensitive topic, and his dismissiveness and skepticism made Perry seem radical or heartless. So many Americans rely on Social Security in old age, and since folks pay into it, they do not believe it is a scam or a welfare program. They may not realize how much poorer the typical American worker is thanks to this scam. Or how unaffordable it is and how much it will rob from young Americans to pay for the elderly, given that the Social Security bank account is practically empty. People are "entitled to their entitlements", so even the so-called conservative Republican base cannot fathom a world without the federal government managing their retirement fund.

But government pension schemes fit the exact definition of a Ponzi scheme. According to the investor site Investopia, a Ponzi scheme is defined as:

Pon · zi scheme *(noun)*

> A fraudulent investing scam promising high rates of return with little risk to investors. The Ponzi scheme generates returns for older investors by acquiring new investors. This scam actually yields the promised returns to earlier investors, as long as there are more new investors. These schemes usually collapse on themselves when the new investments stop.

The only part of this definition that is inconsistent with government pensions is the word "fraudulent." And that is only because the government writes the rules on fraud. It uses force to ensure new investors join the scheme, thereby legitimizing the scam and postponing the collapse. But much like a Ponzi scheme, our government pensions generate returns for older Canadians by requiring new Canadians to join the scheme. The high rates of return promised to seniors come from payments from young taxpayers, rather than the returns of the original investment. Without these new contributors, the Ponzi pension scheme would collapse.

Some fear that seniors are not adequately prepared for retirement, but facts and figures paint a very different picture. The myth that Canadian baby boomers and seniors are unprepared for retirement deserves busting. According to a recent study, the typical baby boomer has about $220,000 saved up in their RRSP. Add to that their government pension and old age benefits, which provide approximately $13,000 per year, or $22,500 for those who also collect GIS. Tax benefits and additional government programs mean that Canadian governments now spend $45,000 a year per senior.[4]

Seniors have experienced huge increases in their wealth and well-being in Canada over the past few decades. Their incomes and wealth continue to grow faster than that of younger Canadians, and their wealth has quadrupled since the 1980s. According to a recent Maclean's cover story, Canadian seniors over the age of 75 make up less than seven per cent of the population, but control more than a third of all financial assets — over $1 trillion. That figure does not include real estate wealth, which has also quadrupled in value since the 1980s.

The truth is, seniors are doing just fine. They are doing better than fine. They are doing very *very* well. So why do politicians keep falling over themselves to please seniors and promise them even more? Why do they continue to hike contribution rates for young taxpayers to top-up CPP payments for rich seniors?

Some politicians are beginning to acknowledge the inevitable failing

---

[4] Maclean's Magazine, "Old and Loaded." September 15, 2014.

of the CPP. But so far, the only politicians brave enough to discuss pension shortfalls — Ontario Premier Kathleen Wynne for instance — want to solve the problem by taking away even more money from young taxpayers. The Ontario Liberal government has introduced a new pension scheme based on the exact same funding model and formula as the CPP. This secondary CPP, called the Ontario Registered Pension Plan (ORPP), will be built on top of the current CPP, and taxpayers will be required to contribute to not just one government Ponzi scheme, but two. This does not address the core problem, that these funds require young people to pay more than they will receive in retirement benefits. The ORPP solution simply takes more money away from taxpayers, and takes away their choice over where to invest their savings. Despite the fact that retirement supplements have long fallen under federal jurisdiction in Canada,[5] starting in 2017, the provincial government in Ontario will begin taxing and meddling in retirement savings. Ontario taxpayers and their employers will together contribute an additional four per cent of their income into this fund. Instead of helping people retire better, this scheme will merely ensure that folks have less after-tax money to save and prepare for their own retirement.

By supporting big-government solutions and the welfare state, everyday people begin to believe that the government will always take care of them. Most do not have specific knowledge of how CPP, OAS or GIS work but they believe the government has programs to take care of them in their old age. They have been conditioned to expect the government to take care of them, so they have neglected to take care of themselves. Trust politicians to invent government solutions to government-created problems.

---

[5] With the exception of Quebec, which is exempt from the CPP and manages its own Quebec Pension Plan

HEALTH CARE

"Early efforts by Western democracies to restrict freedom of contract were rationalized on the grounds that such restrictions were necessary to prevent the suffering of ordinary citizens. People who oppose the freedom to opt out of state-run health insurance schemes turn that rationale on its head: they oppose freedom of contract even when it is necessary to prevent the suffering of ordinary citizens."

— Dr. Jacques Chaoulli

According to polling and popular culture, most Canadians are quite fond of our country's health care system. Some actually associate it with our national character and identity. Perhaps they watched a Michael Moore movie and felt smug and vindicated by the perception that Canadians take better care of one another. Or perhaps it is a hallmark of a rich developed country like Canada to waste billions in a system that makes us feel good about ourselves. Regardless of the motive, Canadians overwhelmingly support the status quo of government health care. Insofar as pensions are considered the "third rail" of politics in Canada, with little hope of reform given the lack of political upside, health care is even more untouchable. It is the sacred cow of Canadian politics.

There are many outspoken critics of our system. And there is no shortage of reasons to be critical. But somehow these criticisms do not translate into the political arena. Suggesting reforms to our government monopoly health care system is treated as a crime worse than treason. As much as some conservative or economic-minded politicians may dislike the system or oppose the state monopoly, they would likely lose their jobs if they become too vocal. Stockwell Day and the Canadian Alliance learned this lesson the hard way during the 2000 federal election campaign. A front-page headline in the Globe and Mail quoted a senior Alliance member saying the party would definitely introduce two-tiered health care. (Two-tier describes the model common in Europe, in which the government system is mirrored by a private system, and patients have the choice between the two options. Sort of like in education, where parents have the choice between government-run public schools or the independent private school system.) The response to the Canadian Alliance was visceral. It was considered the biggest gaffe of the campaign. So much so that during the televised leaders' debate, Stockwell Day held up a hand-written sign saying "NO 2 TIER HEALTH CARE" — a plea to Canadians that his party did not have a secret agenda to offer a choice in health care.

But regardless of this pro-government groupthink among Canada's establishment elites, the days are numbered for our universal government health care system. True, no politician will touch this issue with a 10-foot pole (with the exception of the Wildrose Party in Alberta, whose 2012 election platform included a "Health Care Wait Time Guarantee" which offered a glimmer of hope for choice in Alberta). Luckily for politicians, they will likely be off the hook. They will not be forced to persuade Canadians that choice and competition are better than equality and mediocrity. This is because there are two significant non-political influences working against our struggling health care system that will eventually lead to drastic reforms. These two drivers of change will be discussed in this chapter.

The two prevailing forces are first, the affordability and second, the constitutionality of our system. These two issues are connected and intertwined. As we experience the great demographic shift, the strains on our health care system expose the weak structure, soaring costs and lack of affordability based, again, on economic assumptions that have not panned out. Baby boomers are now retiring, people are living longer, our population is aging and the sustained declining birth rate means our workforce is getting smaller. Because of this shift, our health care system is more heavily utilized and more strained. Unlike a free market that uses the price system to allocate scarce resources, the health care economy deals with scarcity on the basis of first-come first-serve. Health care costs are skyrocketing, and are projected to soar faster than any other government program in the country. To deal with the excess demand of health related services, governments limit the supply through quotas and caps, and thereby create health care queues. Patients are forced to wait for services and often while in pain.

Occasionally, the rationing of care will lead to cause a Canadian patient to die in the health care queue. This is sadly how affordability is linked to the constitutionality of government health care in Canada. It is clearly unconstitutional to force someone to die for the good of big government. But this happens because Canadians are often prohibited from seeking alternative health care when the public queue is too long. Quebec has pioneered a fight for change; in 2006, the Supreme Court found that it was indeed a violation of the Quebec Charter to force people to suffer while waiting for limited government health care services. To deal with the dilemma of people dying in queue, governments allocate more and more funds to the health care system, which takes up an increasing portion of our provincial budgets. (Health care falls under the jurisdiction of the provinces; however, much of its funding comes through federal transfers of tax money.) Despite the acrimony towards opening up our health care system, the weight of the system and all its unintended consequences will give light to a new system that is freer and fairer.

The National Myth

It can be argued that the pioneers of universal health care in Canada were fighting for a noble cause. Tommy Douglas, the original NDP Leader, former Saskatchewan Premier and winner of the CBC popularity contest *The Greatest Canadian,* was an early crusader for health care access and reform. Keep in mind; Tommy Douglas was fighting for universal *access.* Not a government monopoly. He simply believed an individual too poor to afford hospital care should not be turned away to die on the streets. Somehow, the fight for government to protect the least well-off turned into a political bidding war, in which parties fell over each other to offer more goodies at the expense of the invisible taxpayer. Universal access turned into government insurance and then government facilities. The state takeover didn't stop there, and by the 1960s, Canada's health care economy had been nationalized. The ideology of big government and the welfare state had subsumed the entire market, to the point where private coverage became illegal.

> "Canada has historically maintained one of the world's most rigid state-run health care schemes."
>
> — Dr. Jacques Chaoulli

The government response to the overwhelming demand in the health care market is to limit supply, ration care procedures and force queues. Since this rationing of care threatens the image of the government's monopoly, the response is to throw ever more money at the problem. And that's what governments have done.

Our current system was designed in the 1960s; its funding model, like all welfare state inventions, is based on a number of assumptions about growth that have not panned out. And the demographic shift of aging baby boomers will cause a tidal wave in health care spending that has the potential to drown the entire government. Just like pensions, our health care system is another pay-as-you-go model that relies on current taxpayers to pay for a system mostly utilized by the elderly. Among the many demographic and economic changes that have occurred over the past half-century, perhaps the most significant to health care costs is life expectancy. Canadians are living much longer lives, and therefore utilizing the scarce resources of our health care system for many more years than the typical Canadian in the 1960s. It is a great accomplishment of our civilization that people are living into their 80s, 90s, and even 100s. This is cause for celebration. But it also cause for concern when thinking about how to pay for a system in which people are encouraged to retire in their 50s and then go on to live to age 100. We are encouraging people to spend a significant portion of their lives living off the government; living off the taxpayers. This is a terrible policy outcome.

The early assumption that helped perpetuate Canada's government health care system was that the population growth of the post-Second World War baby boom would continue. But, as we know, it has not. And the demographic challenge has a significant effect on our health care system. According to economist Don Drummond, our health care system is projected to soar to consume 80 per cent of total program spending by 2030. And because we are not as rich as we were projected to be, and because our population has not grown as fast was projected, individual taxpayers bear a larger burden of health care costs. Unlike an insurance plan in which younger, healthier individuals pay a monthly premium that is invested and used down the road when they may need care, the pay-as-you-go system uses present-day tax dollars to fund the system. We do not have an investment fund. Every procedure must be budgeted each year. And when those nine million Canadians retire over the next 20 years, it will be up to *generation screwed* to pay the enormous tab for their medical bills.

The sheer complication of trying to plan the health care economy in Canada is dizzying. Not only do we have to predict all the annual procedures and surgeries in a given year, we also have to create a budget and try to stick with it. I can only imagine the logistical nightmare for the central planners. But before you feel badly for the bureaucrats who manage our Byzantine system, remember, you are the ones forced to pay for it. Not only will your tax dollars go towards an inefficient government system with costs projected to soar to cover the increasingly aging population, but also the system may collapse before you ever get to cash in and collect. Since our health care system is not financially sustainable as is, it is unlikely to expected growth spurt in health spending.

In 2013, the total health spending in Canada was about $211 billion, which works out to $5,988 per person. This number has more than doubled since 2000. Of this total expenditure, $141 billion comes from taxpayers, or $8,497 per taxpayer. You are expected to shell out $8,497 in taxes just to pay for health care. Canadians on average fork out another $2,006 per year towards health care through private insurance and out-of-pocket costs for items not covered by Canada's Medicare system, such as prescription drugs, vision care, dental care, physiotherapy and so on. Health care spending is finally starting to slow, after rising at an average rate of seven per cent per year from 2000 to 2010.

You are forking out more than $10,500 each year for health care, but again, just like with pensions, that money is not for you or your own care. It does not go into pre-funding or a savings account with your name or birth year to ensure you get the best care in your aging years after paying such a high premium each year. Instead, it merely goes out the door to pay for this year's health care burden. So if the system ever collapses, or politicians are forced to allow private competition, you will not get any of your money back. Despite years of paying more into the system than you ever use, you will very likely have to pay out of pocket for care in your old age.

Every taxpayer contributes, but as you would expect, we do not use it equally. The typical Canadian uses very little health care after the age of one and before the age of 65. In fact, you will not use as much as you've contributed until after you reach the age of 80. In 2011, the latest year this data breakdown is available, health care spending across age groups is as follows (remember, you pay about $10,500 each year into the system):

Average Healthcare Cost per Person by Age Group

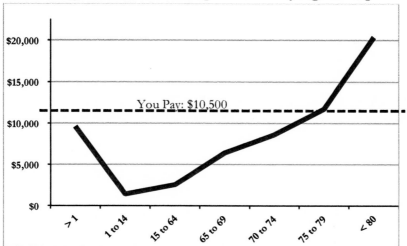

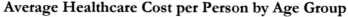

Source: Canadian Institute for Health Information (CIHI), National Health Expenditure Trends, 1975-2013. Figure 34: Provincial/Territorial Government Health Expenditure per capita, by Age Group, 2011

Canada's largest population group, the baby boomers, are starting to turn 65, and will begin to burn through more and more health care dollars. Instead of the baby boomers' contributions from their working years going toward their own benefits (which would make sense, so that funding reflected the size of the cohort), they will rely on *generation screwed*, a significantly smaller group, to pay their health care bills.

For this reason, the health care setup is much like the pension scam; they are both Ponzi schemes. And like pensions, there are "unfunded liabilities" because we do not have enough money in the bank to meet all the promises and future payment obligations owed.

Health care spending is rapidly expanding to reflect the new demographic realities. The government monopoly will bankrupt the entire system if we do not either figure out a way to scale back spending or significantly raise taxes. When the government monopoly was designed, the portion of Canadians over the age of 65 was 7.7 per cent. By 2000, that had increased to 12.5 per cent, and in 2011 it was 14.5 per cent. That ratio is expected to reach a whopping 24.7 per cent by 2051, around the time I would retire. Given that most health care expenditures are on folks over 65 (which is also the group that may no longer be net-contributors of taxes to the government), this is more than a problem. It is a catastrophe. Just around the corner.

Chaoulli v. Quebec

Quebec may appear to be unlikely grounds for the rebellion against government and the first province to champion the cause of private health care. But big government oppression drives unpredictable outcomes from citizens. In Quebec, the story began with a 73-year-old salesman named George Zeliotis. Mr. Zeliotis was suffering while waiting for hip replacement surgery, and he became an activist for reducing Quebec hospital wait times. In 1996, he had waited an entire year in queue for his surgery. He was in pain and asked the government hospitals if he could pay directly for this surgery in order to skip the public queue. He wasn't a rich man, just a desperate one. He learned that it was against the law to pay for surgery in Canada, and decided to take his case to court. Canadians can buy private insurance for health care that falls outside the government Medicare system, such as prescriptions, dental care, physiotherapy, or even private hospital rooms. But paying for something that the government does offer is illegal. Mr. Zeliotis argued that forcing Canadians to wait an entire year for surgery was unreasonable, endangered his life and infringed on the Charter's guarantee of the right to life, liberty and security.

While George Zeliotis argued his case and made his way through the courts, another man was fighting a similar battle. Dr. Jacques Chaoulli is a French-born physician who provided home appointments and applied for a license to offer some services also provided by Medicare. His applications were rejected on the grounds of provincial legislation banning private health insurance, which prevents doctors who do not operate within the Medicare plan from charging patients for services. Dr. Chaoulli also decided to challenge this decision through the courts, and became an activist for a two-tiered, public-private system as is common in Western Europe.

Despite having separate complaints, the court decided to hear the two plaintiffs together. The men lost in two Quebec provincial courts, but were able to appeal and get their case heard before the Supreme Court of Canada. While the plaintiffs were fighting for the individual rights and freedoms of Canadians not to suffer or die because of government policy, the government lawyers argued that the court should not interfere with the health care monopoly because it is considered "one of Canada's finest achievements and a powerful symbol of the national identity." Pride of big government trumps individual liberty, they argued.

In June 2005, the Supreme Court struck down the Quebec law banning private care. The 4-3 decision ruled that the *Quebec Health Insurance Act* and the *Hospital Insurance Act* that bans private health care in Quebec violate Quebec's *Charter of Rights and Freedoms*. Three judges also found that it violates the Canadian *Charter of Rights and Freedoms*, in a split 3-3 decision (one judge abstained). The long wait times were found to violate the right to life and security of person. With this ruling, Quebec's government monopoly on health care was dealt a serious blow, giving Quebeckers the option of private insurance when the government system cannot provide the care they need.

The decision was not enough to put an end to the state monopoly, but it was a step in the right direction toward a better system. The ruling was complex, as it only applies under certain circumstances and only applies in Quebec. It will continue to be a long battle to establish an affordable and fair market for health care, but the Chaoulli case certainly created a legal pathway toward change. Many legal experts and activists believe it is only a matter of time before the same challenges are made in other provinces (similar cases are currently making their way through the courts in both Alberta and British Columbia), and all Canadians are granted the constitutional right not to suffer for the sake of big government.

GOVERNMENT WORKERS

"The only thing that saves us from the bureaucracy is its inefficiency."

— Eugene McCarthy, former US Senator and poet

"Bureaucracy expands to meet the needs of the expanding bureaucracy."

— Oscar Wilde

"Every revolution evaporates and leaves behind only the slime of a new bureaucracy."

— Franz Kafka

As politicians made endless promises and thereby built the modern day welfare state, the government had to go on a hiring frenzy to staff all the central planners needed to fulfill all the big promises. Alongside all the entitlements of the welfare state came the need for hundreds of thousands of government employees. Somebody needs to push paper around and administer all the new programs. But as more Canadians began to work for the government, fewer remained as net-taxpaying citizens; the ones needed to fund all the big promises. It's a bit of a catch-22: the bigger the government, the more money needed to administer it, but fewer people remaining to pay taxes. And with higher administration costs, fewer funds are left available to actually pay for the welfare state. More money to fat-cat unions, and less to actual social programs.

This chapter will chronicle the multiplication of government employees alongside the growth in government. It is not just salaries that drive up the costs of government, but the many benefits that are burdensome for taxpayers and particularly for *generation screwed*.

Recent Statistics Canada figures show that 21.8 per cent of people working in Canada are employees of the government. In Manitoba, it's much higher at 27 per cent. More than one in five Canadians workers is government-employed. More than one in four workers in Manitoba is a government worker. Not only do we have to pay for all the big promises, we also have to pay the salaries of 21.8 per cent of the entire workforce. And the picture of who is actually funding all this government is bleaker than it first appears. According to the National Household Survey, Canada's total employment rate is 60.9 per cent per cent, or 16,595,035 of the 34 million Canadian citizens and permanent residents. Of the 16.6 million Canadian workers (again according to the latest data available), 3,631,837 people work in the broad government sector: federal, provincial, territorial, municipal, school boards, health and social service institutes, universities, colleges, trade schools, and state-owned enterprises. This leaves 12,963,198 net-contributing taxpayers, or 37.03 per cent of the total population. Or fewer than four tax "payers" for each tax "receiver". Those taxpayers will pay for the growing costs of big government and the welfare state. And young workers will bear an even larger burden.

The programs discussed in the last two chapters — pensions and health care — are designed to benefit everyone, even if our politicians' hearts were bigger than their government wallets. This chapter, on the other hand, paints the picture of an elite club of "haves" who needn't worry about their retirement savings or about the strength of the economy. These elites are guaranteed their riches, regardless of the economy or the health of their pension funds. Canada's real elites are government employees; these folks receive some of the most lucrative benefit packages and gold-plated pension deals in the economy. Forget about the poor vs. the rich. The real divide in Canada is between the four taxpayers who contribute so that each government employee can collect.

Paying the salaries of employees is the single largest expense in government. Not health care. Not education. Bureaucrats. About 30 cents of every tax dollar spent by the federal government goes to government operating costs including salaries, benefits, supplies, and travel. In Ontario, the number is much higher: 50 per cent of all money sent to Queen's Park goes to government employee compensation. The same can be said for just about any government in Canada. Many government departments, such as education for example, commit more than 70 per cent of their total budget to employee compensation. And any guesses as to what represents the biggest driver of health care expenditures? It is not the aging population or care for older seniors. The largest increase in the past decade was actually the compensation of health care workers. So as we try to pinch every penny to make it last to cover our aging population, unions representing health care workers are demanding a larger and larger slice of the pie for their employees.

Government unions are an important player in the scheme of big government; they empower their own special interests, in this case government employees. Taxpayers be damned. Forced dues from members fund government-sector unions in Canada. Membership is mandatory, so all government employees become dues-paying members. There are very few rules governing how pooled union dues are spent, so union leadership typically funnel vast amounts of money to politicians who promise the best deal for fat-cat union bosses and their members. These are the type of deals exposed by James Buchanan's Public Choice Theory, discussed in Part One, demonstrating how politicians are prone to engage in deals that benefit some at the expense of others. Politicians are promised union votes needed to win office; in exchange, union leaders and members are promised more money and benefits. And you the taxpayer? You are left with the bill.

This exchange of favours tells part of the story of how unions help to elect pro-union parties, which has led to the growth in the government sector and continual growth in lucrative compensation packages for government employees. Self-preservation of big government is a top concern for all government employees, so unions do their part to ensure that only status–quo, big-government politicians, in parties of all stripes, are allowed to govern. Anyone who thinks this might be untrue or unfair need merely look at Ontario, and the 22 unions which ran anti-PC and anti-Tim Hudak campaigns in the 2014 provincial election. A typical election features two, three or sometimes four parties running campaigns and political ads. In Ontario, limited laws regulating third-party advertisements were exploited by shameless unions, which become partisan stooges when union jobs are at risk. Tens of millions of dollars were spent on political campaign ads to stop the PC plan to eliminate 100,000 government jobs.

As big government has grown, so too have these powerful unions and the corresponding price tag. Working for the government once meant earning less money than a job in the private sector, in exchange for a greater sense of service and increased job security. The very phrase "civil servant" implies that bureaucrats are not self-interested, but instead exist to serve the public. This romantic notion of the bureaucracy is a fairy tale. Unions and their members are just as self-interested as any workers in the economy. They want more money and more lucrative benefits for themselves.

And they have achieved many of their demands. Salary growth in the government sector has turned this notion on its head. In Ontario, government employees earn about 14 per cent more than their non-government counterparts in similar positions, according to a report by the Fraser Institute. Government employees still receive more job security, as few ever lose their jobs regardless of performance or conduct, but they also receive other perks: shorter hours, more paid sick days, more vacation time and early retirement. The typical government bureaucrat retires three years earlier than the typical Canadian worker, and eight years prior to the new official retirement age of 67. Some still receive the incredible benefit of "sick day banks," under which employees can bank unused sick days and use them to supplement a longer vacation next year, or cash out the value upon retirement like a secondary pension. Being a government employee is a sweet gig.

Ontario leads the country in terms of the data it makes public on government workers. Each year, it proactively releases its annual "Sunshine List" — a list of all government employees who earn more than $100,000 annually in salary and personal expenses. This list is a microcosm of government growth across the country, particularly the growth in the number of well-paid middle managers.

Number of Government Employees on Ontario's Sunshine List

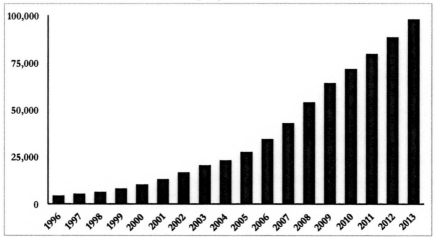

Source: Government of Ontario, Public Sector Salary Disclosure, Ministry of Finance. Released March 28, 2014.

As the number of government employees grows and each individual employee grows richer, the tax burden on non-government sectors increases, and so too does the increasing inequality between those who work for the government and everyone else. Taxpayers pay government employees for perks they themselves do not receive. Higher salaries, more sick leave and vacation days, fewer hours, more job security and earlier retirement. But there is another perk that government workers receive that taxpayers couldn't dream of: lucrative pensions.

While only 24 per cent of private sector employees have a registered workplace pension plan, 87 per cent of government workers do; the vast majority of these are the most lucrative and costly: defined-benefit pension plans indexed to inflation. These plans guarantee stated retirement benefits regardless of the health of the pension fund. Government workers will receive the pension benefits laid out in their contracts, no matter how much (or how little) money they contribute, the rate of inflation, how well their money is invested by fund managers, how the markets perform, how early they retire or how long they live. These government employees are typically promised and entitled to three-quarters of maximum career salary each year for their entire life. These are known as "defined-benefit" pension plans, and they are all but extinct outside the government.

Many government pension funds are headed full steam toward insolvency, for exactly the same reasons that CPP, OAS and Medicare costs are skyrocketing. As the largest age group in our population retires and begin to collect benefits, the smaller number of remaining workers will have to contribute more and more. In the case of government sector pensions, the "employer" contributions come from taxpayers. So the preferred option to maintain the health of any fund is to increase contributions, meaning taxpayers fork over more and more. This still has not been enough to keep pace with the demands from retirees collecting defined benefit pensions, so taxpayers are again on the hook to bail out these funds. Government employees will receive their benefits even if their pension fund is completely empty and taxpayers have to pay their retirement salary directly.

Any shortfalls to the fund are topped up and paid by taxpayers through sneaky bailouts called "special contributions." According to Statistics Canada data compiled by the Canadian Taxpayers Federation, taxpayers across Canada contributed $18.1 billion into government employee pension plans in 2012. This is almost three times more than the $6.7 billion paid back in 2002. Taxpayers are forking over billions each year to top up the bankrupt government pension schemes, leaving taxpayers with less to save for their own retirement. This represents the largest bailout using taxpayer dollars in Canadian history. Where are the protests?

Instead of acknowledging this problem, politicians continue to appease fat cat union bosses, and hide pension shortfalls by quietly increasing "employer" contributions – another way of saying taxpayers get stuck with the bill.

This happens all across Canada, at all levels of government. According to a recent study by Mark Milke of the Fraser Institute, the following pensions have been given stealth bailouts:

• In Alberta in 2002, the province made what was supposed to be a one-time payment of $60 million towards funding shortfalls for the so-called 'pre-1992' Teachers' Pension Plan. It took over that liability completely in 2007 and made another payment of $1.2 billion to the same fund in 2009.

• In Newfoundland and Labrador, several pension plans have required topping up, including a $2-billion special payment into the Teachers' Pension Plan in 2006 and $982 million for the Public Service Pension Plan in 2007.

• In Ontario, the province has made special annual payments of $416 million towards funding shortfalls in the Public Service Pension Plan since 2007. The province is scheduled to make payments of $142 million per year for 15 years.

Taxpayers and non-government workers are on the hook for the lavish retirement funds and golden parachutes of the government class. So while many may complain about the gap between rich and poor, or the 1 per cent and the 99 per cent, the real injustice in our economy is the divide between the government class and its under-lords, the taxpayers. The 37 per cent. We are on the hook for making sure the rich stay rich in their retirement, while *generation screwed* struggles to keep the whole system afloat.

EVERYTHING ELSE

"Every step and every movement of the multitude, even in what are termed enlightenment ages, are made with equal blindness to the future; and nations stumble upon establishments, which are indeed the result of human action, but not the execution of any human design."

— Adam Ferguson, 1782

The moral of this story is that the political world around us is about to change. All the assumptions that served as the foundation of our political economy are fatally flawed. Our foundation is cracked and the house is sinking. As the numbers demonstrate, our social entitlements under the welfare state are not properly funded. The assumptions about growth from the 1950s, 60s and 70s have not held up, and as our economy and population cease to grow, so too can our expectations and demands from government. We will experience real change in our lifetime, as the welfare state slowly collapses. This change will force us to re-examine all the assumptions about our system.

For instance, many of Canada's labour policies were designed in the era when baby boomers were first joining the labour market. And it shows. Many of these policies actually encourage people not to work!

During the initial baby boom, interventionist economists were worried that the economy wasn't big enough and wouldn't grow fast enough to accommodate all the new workers entering the work force. Many of these labour policies — like welfare, EI and pensions — actually provide incentives that encourage staying at home or retiring early. They policies are actually designed with the objective of taking people *out* of the workforce. And while the economy was growing and booming, the government was collecting enough to pay the benefits and entitlements of all those out-of-work people. That is obviously no longer the case. We now have the opposite problem. We need workers, and even more so, we need taxpayers. We can no longer afford these costly labour market policies that cause governments to run annual deficits to keep their heads above water. This chapter will discuss some of the other policies that no longer make sense and need to be adjusted to reflect the new realities of *generation screwed.*

While government welfare programs provide incentives for individuals not to work, big government encourages people to work for the government. Government itself is the largest make-work program, and given the compensation packages they offer in this economy, recruiting talent has never been easier. After subsidizing all those liberal arts degrees, the government then hires many of those grads to come work for them, pushing papers around, running dockets from the 20th floor up to the 21st floor and back down, and generally doing busywork at a nine-to-five job. The government would rather employ these people than pay them to sit at home and feel unhappy. So the government hires them. The government also poaches people from the private economy, often offering better compensation packages and less work. The government takes people out of the wealth-producing sector and sucks them into the wealth-consuming sector. Something is seriously wrong with this. The entire idea of a government sector pulling wealth from the economy and squandering it on social experiments and make-work projects is entirely wrong and entirely unaffordable.

In order for our government Ponzi schemes to perpetuate and be fully funded, we need more workers and more people in the economy. We need bodies. People willing to work, pay taxes and conform to the status quo (without asking too many questions). And because we desperately need workers, Canada welcomes more immigrants per capita than any other country in the world. We currently maintain the highest sustained levels of immigration in our history. This is a virtue; our country is far wealthier, productive and interesting because of sustained immigration. But even if we doubled or tripled those numbers, it would not be enough to reverse the trend of mass retirement and unfunded liabilities. Immigration simply isn't enough to tilt the scales and fix the math. It can help, and Canada is very lucky in that so many people want to come here. We are also fortunate that all of our country's major political parties are pro-immigration and support pluralism. We benefit enormously from welcoming skilled and ambitious workers from around the world, and we should continue to welcome as many workers into our economy as possible; especially if we want to be better able to pay for the burden of big government and big promises.

Other things are changing as baby boomers retire, aside from our inability to pay for big government. Many baby boomers are selling their homes in the suburbs and moving back into revitalized urban cores. Canada is a highly urban population, and as many new Canadians are settling in our major cities, baby boomers are moving back downtown, and many young families are not leaving. Instead of following in their parents' footsteps and moving to the 'burbs to have children, many young families are remaining in the cities.

This is wreaking havoc on central planners in municipal

governments. The outdated urban planning model is based on people living in the periphery and commuting to the city's core. Most infrastructure and taxpayer-funded investments are based on this model. But as more people live closer to the core, more people have reverse commutes, unconventional hours or even work from home. They have different needs and demands. The demands met by markets are quickly accommodated, like grocery stores, medical clinics, dentists, restaurants, cafes, drug stores, gyms, dry cleaners and so on. The demands met by the government are at a standstill. Unionized construction workers clog Canadian streets during the summer, as city council grants too many building permits and our streets resemble war zones during the few warm months of the year. There are often too few schools, parks and sidewalks. And not enough parking spaces to accommodate all the new residents. And while the politicians undertake costly transit projects to bring more people into cities from neighbouring suburbs, there is not enough transit to get people around downtown. Our cities are broken and need fixing.

And our housing system also works against young people. Baby boomers and older generations were able to buy homes for a portion of their income, and then sit back and watch the value grow exponentially over the years, serving as a great investment that equates to a secondary retirement fund for homeowners. Most young people, on the other hand, cannot afford to buy real estate anywhere in the country, and especially not in cities. They are forced to rent for the first several years of their career. They are simply paying the mortgage of an older worker. Instead of money being transferred down to future generations, it is still being funnelled back up to older and richer generations.

As techies and engineers are coding away, and private investors are spending billions of private money to develop a self-driving car, the government is still using central planners to design and impose 19th century transportation policy (trains, bicycles) and stubbornly refusing to enable 20th century transportation (automobiles). Which would you chose: to commute to a train station, then wait for the train according to the government's schedule, then board an uncomfortable public train, only to disembark and commute again from the train station to your office? Or, to use a Google self-driving car, that will pick you up at your doorstep and drop you off wherever you need to go, while costs are driven down with rideshare and carpooling. The choice is self-evident, and yet, the government is hell-bent on developing more rail and more out-dated public transit models.

Toronto, for instance, is moving forward on its plan for "The Big Move." Bureaucrats likely lifted the name, however ironically, from Boston's "Big Dig" project; a public policy nightmare to redesign traffic flow in Boston that has taken the better part of a century, cost trillions, and is still incomplete. Toronto plans to spend the next 25 years and 50 billion taxpayer dollars to promote suburban sprawl and build subways to connect every suburb, exurb and commuter city, from Peterborough to Kitchener, Hamilton to Barrie with government transit and rail. One can only imagine the technological breakthroughs that will be witnessed by 2040 that will make the idea of government rail even more obsolete. The government's stubborn attachment to rail is beyond irresponsible. It's obsessive-compulsive.

Instead of squandering other people's money on out-dated ideas, the kind of change we need should focus on individuals and spontaneous order. We need labour reforms to keep people in the economy longer, not enable them to retire early or allow able-bodied workers to sit at home because the government will pay them to be there. We simply cannot afford it.

GENERATION SCREWED RECAP

Don't worry. There is no exam. It is important, however, to arm yourself with the facts about *generation screwed*. This is an overview of what we've learned so far, and all the problems you are about to inherit. Here are the Five Ws on *generation screwed*.

Who:

Generation screwed is the generation of young Canadians — everyone younger than the baby boomer generation, but more specifically, *Millennials* or people born after 1980 — who will bear the burden of the previous generation's reckless fiscal management.

What:

Older Canadians voted to expand social entitlement programs and the size of government. They also allowed governments to borrow and use debt to finance much of the cost of government benefits. Young Canadians are therefore set to inherit both large social programs that eat up a significant portion of their paycheque in taxes, as well as a debt burden accumulated over the past half century by governments that don't pay their bills.

Specifically, *generation screwed* is set to inherit:

- $1.2 trillion in combined federal and provincial net debt

- Gross debt that equates to 87 per cent of Canada's GDP

- Compound interest (meaning we pay interest on the interest of government debt)

- Skyrocketing cost of "servicing" the debt eating up more and more of our government finances

- Another $2.9 trillion in unfunded liabilities, or government promises that do not have funds set aside and will therefore cause future debt

- Health care costs, elderly benefits, social assistance and pensions that are not pre-funded, and will draw funds from annual budgets

- Growing costs for government employee compensation and benefits

- Dozens of heavily indebted government sector pension funds that require annual bailouts

- An expanding government bureaucracy to meet the needs of a society overly dependent on government programs

- Increasing demands from powerful and self-interested government sector unions

- Premium hikes for programs like the Canada Pension Plan (CPP) and Employment Insurance (EI)

- Record high levels of personal debt, encouraged by risky government monetary policies like stimulus, quantitative easing and artificially low interest rates

- An increasingly stagnant economy, lower wages and a real drop in the standard of living for *generation screwed*

- A shrinking working-aged population due to the large scale exodus from the workforce by baby boomers

- Fewer taxpayers to carry a larger tax burden

- Further cost increases to fund health care, elderly benefits, social assistance and pensions as the population ages

- $45,000 a year per senior in program spending and special tax breaks, courtesy of Canadian taxpayers

- Continual tax hikes and reduced benefits for *generation screwed*

When:

We are experiencing a critical shift in our country's demographics. As Canada's population ages, and baby boomers retire, our public finances will reach a tipping point. Soon, as many people will receive government benefits as those paying into the system through contributions. The is a double whammy for public finances. First, the largest cohort of Canadians will leave the workforce; many will no longer be net-contributing taxpayers. Second, these folks will begin to collect and utilize the most expensive forms of social assistance in our society: pensions, old age benefits and healthcare. As these social programs become more utilized and strained, more funding will be required to cover the tab. This means young Canadians will face premium hikes and tax increases to pay for programs that have been chronically under-funded.

Where:

This phenomenon is not unique to Canada (although this book is based on the Canadian experience.) Across the West, big promises made by politicians have drastically expanded what political scientists call the *welfare state*. This system of government provides a social safety net and an imposed minimum standard of living for all citizens. No matter your place in society, everyone has access to free social entitlements, like education, health care, social assistance, employment insurance and a basic pension. Should they need it, all Canadians also have access to government housing, basic income, and food and drug subsidies.

What were originally programs intended only for the very poor and needy, welfare state programs have morphed over the past century and now provide extensive government services for everyone. The middle class is the largest voting block in society, and they also became the greatest recipients of government spending. But this has lead to an overload on the system and a strain on public finances across Western liberal democracies. The government has overextended itself, and it is now failing at its core functions.

Why:

This book argues that the problem lies at the very core of our model of government. Short-term thinking is promoted by short election cycles and an even shorter news cycle. Politicians make big promises to citizens in order to win office — without properly calculating the costs of their promises. Economists and bankers also promote this short-term thinking by encouraging and allowing governments to borrow and accumulate debt. This debt is passed on to future taxpayers and citizens, who are forced to pay for the social programs of past generations, as well as the annual costs of servicing the debt and paying interest. We are heavily reliant on debt. Without it, the entire system would come tumbling down. But sooner or later (and this book predicts sooner) our debt will be called in, and we will have to wake up to the fact that the big promises of the welfare state are merely an illusion. They are not real. Big promises like "free" education, health care, social assistance, pensions and a government that provides lucrative employment for one-fifth of our population is not financially sustainable and cannot last. We are not rich enough to pay the bill. Instead, our government has relied on borrowing, and intends to pass that debt to the next generation of taxpayers; to *generation screwed.*

Young Canadians deserve better, and this book encourages *generation screwed* to reject the schemes handed to them and demand a better deal.

PART V

THE SOLUTION

"A pessimist sees difficulty in every opportunity.
An optimist sees opportunity in every difficulty."

— Winston Churchill

The problems laid out in this book are incredibly complex; their solutions will not come easily. Our society's dependency has been instilled over generations, and it may take even longer to overcome this dependency. Difficult problems require complex solutions. But change is inevitable, and *generation screwed* has an opportunity to build something better.

Many skeptics fear that the trends outlined in this book will lead to some pretty bleak outcomes. They predict that mass dependency on government will cause the government to continue to grow — and take over more and more of the economy in order to pay for all the entitlement programs. The continual government growth will cause the economy to contract because of escalating taxes, and reduce our standard of living in the process. This phenomenon will eventually lead to government defaults and bankruptcy, meaning the government will be unable to pay its bills and send out all those government cheques to all the dependent people. When pensioners stop receiving their cheques, there will be chaos, rioting for entitlements, and perhaps ultimately, a breakdown of law and order, as our social contract erodes. This perhaps sounds shocking and alarmist. But this is essentially what happened in Greece. Because it was only one country in chaos, others were able and willing to bail them out. But what if everyone defaults? Who will bail out Ontario? The feds cannot step in if they themselves are being crushed by rising spending and out-of-control debt. If Canada, the US and Western Europe are all struggling to keep their heads above water, who is left to bail us out? Saudis? Chinese? I don't think anyone wants to imagine what the future looks like under these scenarios. But it doesn't look bright if we continue down the path of more debt and borrowing to pay for all the promises of the welfare state.

I trust that by reading this far, you are quite concerned about the state of our government and economy here in Canada. I hope that you agree: something must be done. We must change course. But this will be no easy task. As I've said throughout this book, reforming our political and economic systems will be the biggest challenge of our generation. In many ways, this also leaves us with a tremendous opportunity to be at the table during these reforms, and ensure that whatever we come up with, it is a system that is more fair and free for everyone.

I started the book on a positive note, with my own personal experiences coming to my free market views and the excitement of being a young libertarian. I also intend to end on a similarly positive note. Leading Enlightenment-era philosopher John Locke was an optimist when it comes to human nature. He believed that people were rational, capable of independent thought and intrinsically endowed with free will and liberty. I am with John Locke on this one, and so were the US founding fathers when they drafted the founding documents and institutions of America. I believe that human

163

innovation and logic are capable of solving the world's most challenging problems.

Professor Tyler Cowen argues that big government was able to grow only because of advances and growth in the economy, and similarly, the government cannot continue to grow without corresponding growth the economy. Many politicians haven't quite figured this out yet, and so they try to use debt and borrowing schemes to finance government growth beyond the economy. This cannot go on forever. Eventually, the lenders or the taxpayers will say enough is enough. No more borrowing. No more fake growth. No more intergenerational theft.

But short of bankruptcy and defaults, how can *generation screwed* wake up their peers and politicians to the unsustainable and unfair foundation of the welfare state? To quote Thomas Jefferson, "the tree of liberty must be refreshed from time to time with the blood of patriots and tyrants." And while I do not agree that blood needs to run in order to enact social change, Jefferson's quote can be interpreted as a metaphor for the fury of citizen advocacy and lawful activism; of the people demanding more respect and a better deal from their government. Unlike our American neighbours, Canada has a strong history of peaceful change, as we achieved independence from British rule through polite, gentlemanly meetings and the stroke of a pen. Canada has a uniquely strong tradition of peaceful reforms towards increased freedom. As with the end of imperial rule, the collapses of big government will come slowly and inevitably.

Canada is well suited to lead the way. The Canadian parliament was founded on the principles of "peace, order and good government," but our traditions and ancient liberties trace back to the *Magna Carta* of 1215, also known as the *Great Charter of the Liberties of England, and of the Liberties of the Forest*. Many Canadians may point to the 1982

Charter of Rights and Freedoms as the origin of our political rights, but they are overlooking an important part of our established tradition of ordered liberty. As Canadians, in fact, we derive our natural rights through a non-codified natural law, our history of rights dating back to the Magna Carta, and from God.

> "The Magna Carta is the greatest constitutional document of all times — the foundation of the freedom of the individual against the arbitrary authority of the despot."
>
> — Lord Denning

We should remember this important fact about Canada's heritage. Many Canadians, especially conservatives and libertarians, look longingly at the US, its Declaration of Independence and its focus on the inalienable rights, "life, liberty and the pursuit of happiness." Yes, their founding fathers were brilliant. And yes, they took seriously their duty to establish a constitution that recognizes the tyrannical nature of political power, and attempts to protect individuals from the coercive powers of government. The constitution was written knowing full well that human liberty comes first, and governments are merely there to protect our primary rights. But how well is that experiment working now? A constitution is useless if citizens do not share the core principles of individuals before government.

In many ways, we may have the stronger tradition of liberty and freedom, not for what the Magna Carta says explicitly, but for what it implicitly represents. It remains our duty as Canadians to keep this tradition alive, and not let Canada be swallowed by the myths and propaganda perpetuated over the last few decades; that Canada is some kind of a socialist utopia. We are not. We are a country that has a deep and strong tradition of freedom, resourcefulness and capability. Canadians have long held an international reputation for being rowdy, spirited and always willing to fight for what is right.

The final chapters of this book outline some of the solutions for *generation screwed;* both the short-term, through proven public policy solutions, and the longer strategy of establishing and ensuring a free society in Canada, and around the world.

BATTLE OF IDEAS

"We must make the building of a free society once more an intellectual adventure, a deed of courage."

— Friedrich Hayek, *Studies in Philosophy, Politics and Economics, 1967*

"Unless we can make the philosophic foundations of a free society once more a living intellectual issue, and its implementation a task which challenges the ingenuity and imagination of our liveliest minds, the prospects of freedom are indeed dark. But if we can regain that belief in the power of ideas which was the mark of liberalism at its best, the battle is not lost."

— Friedrich Hayek, *Studies in Philosophy, Politics and Economics, 1967*

When it comes to winning the battle of ideas, the broad free market coalition is falling behind in Canada and around the world. To understand how this battle is being lost, we can find a perfect example in the situation in Ottawa with the Harper Conservative government.

By all accounts, Stephen Harper is a thoughtful and highly intelligent free market conservative, who came to his worldview through economics and a close reading of classical liberal scholars such as Hayek and Bastiat. In the 1990s, Harper became disillusioned with the Reform Party because of its social policies, and helped refocus the Reform political movement on economic issues such as reducing the size of government, committing to balanced budgets and paying off the national debt. Harper strongly believed that much of the federal government had become nothing more than activist bureaucracies and massive slush funds; he called for entire departments of the federal government to be eliminated.

So why is it that his Conservative government has run consecutive deficits, driven the country to its highest ever level of debt (in numerical terms), oversaw stimulus spending and the biggest deficit in Canadian history ($50 billion in 2009), administered the auto bailouts, and force-rejected the market sale of Potash Corp to an Australian company? (The justification was fear of an eventual takeover by a Chinese state-owned enterprise, yet he then allowed the sale of Calgary oil and gas giant Nexen directly to CNOOC — the Chinese National Offshore Oil Corporation — a Chinese state-owned enterprise.)

True, I have cherry-picked the economic failures of Harper's regime. There are many achievements of the Harper government that liberty advocates can celebrate, such as the multitude of free trade deals, the elimination of countless slush funds, significant tax reduction, ending the Wheat Board monopoly, scrapping the long-gun registry and eliminating red tape to allow for resource development. We have also seen drastic reforms to our immigration system to allow more people to come to Canada to work, and fewer to come and collect the many social benefits of our welfare state. Harper has even enacted free market reforms that actually left himself and his party less well-off.

His 2012 pension reforms included a significant cut to prime ministerial pensions, personally forgoing millions of dollars over his lifetime. Similarly, his government abolished the political party subsidy, a per-vote payment to political parties following elections. The Conservatives had received the most votes, and therefore lost the most money from the reform.

The reason Stephen Harper has been inconsistent in his policy reforms is simple: at the end of the day, Harper is a politician, and a damned good one. As a politician, his most important goal is to get elected and re-elected. In order to win, you have to gain the approval of a plurality of Canadians and, unfortunately, Canadians are neither consistent in their worldview nor principally in favour of the free market. Canadians are centrists who take inconsistent positions on issues and vary in their opinions on social and fiscal issues. In order to maintain his coalition, Harper cannot be a principled ideologue. He has to govern as a pragmatist and compromise his core beliefs.

Harper governs from the centre, and when he can, he will bring in modest free market reforms. But most of the time, he will just govern in a utilitarian fashion, making decisions that will please the broadest number of people. Stephen Harper is a realist. He understands the limits of his political power and the long-term consequences of imposing free market policies against the will of the general public. If he were to impose free market reforms outlined in this book — reducing the government bureaucracy, opening up and allowing private health care or permitting personalized pension accounts rather than the CPP — it would cause a shock to our political and economic systems.

You need to be a realist to operate in Ottawa as a politician. Ottawa is an odd place, and perhaps it takes working there to really understand it. Many movement conservatives and free market advocates consider working in Ottawa akin to a tour of duty. It can be a very frustrating and disheartening place for someone who opposes the big-government status quo. When I worked for a federal minister, immediately following the 2011 election victory in which the Conservatives achieved a coveted majority government, I learned an incredible amount about the real government; things that could not be taken from a textbook or newspaper. I certainly saw first hand the real pressure and constraints on free market politicians and the various actors that prevent free market policies. Conservatives are the real radicals in Ottawa, and those fighting tooth and nail to maintain the status quo are the left-leaning social democrats: the Liberals and New Democrats. How terribly ironic that the radicals fighting for liberty and change get dubbed "conservative," while those fighting to maintain their place of privilege and control get to call themselves "liberal."

> "All the pleasing illusions, which made power gentle, and obedience liberal, which harmonized the different shades of life, and which, by a bland assimilation, incorporated into politics the sentiments which beautify and soften private society, are to be dissolved by this new conquering empire of light and reason. All the decent drapery of life is to be rudely torn off...their liberty is not liberal."

> — Edmund Burke, French Revolution

The Ottawa Bubble

Imagine you are a libertarian or free market conservative politician or political staffer in Ottawa, and imagine the constraints you face on a daily basis. As press secretary to a minister, I primarily dealt with the media, the bureaucracy, the Prime Minister's Office (PMO), the opposition parties and "stakeholders" (also known as special interest groups). These are the five main groups that make up the Ottawa bubble, and each has its own traits and motives — all of which lead the country further away from the foundations of a free society.

First, the media. They make it no secret that the "mainstream" (or "groupthink") media are no fans of the Harper administration. Consider that the majority of the parliamentary press gallery work for media organizations that receive money from taxpayers or rely on special treatment from the CRTC. The CBC alone makes up a significant portion of the parliamentary press gallery and acts as opinion leader that can very much shape the news cycle. Given its budget and resources — thanks, of course, to the hundreds of millions in annual taxpayer dollar transfers — the CBC can easily lead the charge in chasing stories and breaking news. The news they chase and break, therefore, has a bias, however slight, towards big-government solutions and causes. Journalists in general tend to be more focused on social issues, which are easy to understand and garner more sympathy from the audience, than on economic issues, which may require some math skills or research to understand and cover. Journalists that move to the capital, as with anyone that moves to Ottawa, hold some affinity for, and a general belief in, the power of the federal government. They wouldn't develop an interest in federal issues if they didn't tend to favour federal government solutions and intervention. They are very likely to hold views that support a strong central government.

Media galleries in BC and Alberta, where the governing party rarely, if ever, changes, are used to acting as the "official opposition" to the government. More and more, the parliamentary gallery in Ottawa has also assumed this role. From breaking non-stories, like the "robocall scandal" or the "in-and-out scandal" — which no one outside of the Ottawa bubble knows or cares anything about — the capital's media are obsessed with "process" and personality stories that are easy to tell. They tend to ignore the more important policy stories, which are complex, less sexy and difficult to explain in a quick headline.

The things I learned very quickly as a press secretary in Ottawa:

1) Journalists are very busy; they don't like research or complex stories;

2) They either mistrust conservatives or have a preference for activist government. Given the option of the government doing something or doing nothing, an Ottawa journalist will lean toward intervention. Instead of questioning the role of government, the precedent of federal jurisdiction and the affordability of intervention, most journalists I interacted with in Ottawa always seemed to assume a problem could, and should, be solved by the federal government.

Second, the bureaucracy. It is a given that the bureaucracy itself is very pro-big government. Anyone who goes to work in Ottawa as a political staffer can expect to work with — and work against — the civil service. Career government employees obviously start from a different worldview and persuasion than the typical Canadian. Of course they believe in the federal government's ability to solve incredibly complex problems across the country: why else would they devote their entire lives to working for the federal government? And as discussed in the Big Government chapter, civil servants primarily serve themselves, their own self-interests and their worldview about the role of government. They are not void of self-interest. So they fight for bigger budgets, larger staff, more interventionist policies and programs, more perks and benefits, and generally, for the federal government to do more and play a larger role in the day-to-day lives of Canadians. They love the government! And they fervently believe in its powers. (Either that or they are totally uninterested in politics and work there simply for the perks.)

One of the first concepts I learned in the political science discourse was the law of parliamentary sovereignty. Parliamentary sovereignty — a tradition of British common law — says that no government is bound by the decisions of previous governments. This means that commonwealth governments receive the power to make or unmake any law whatsoever. This concept gave me the impression that each government, when formed, can start anew and govern how it pleases, within the confine of its powers. In practice, at least in Ottawa, this is far from the case. Change is very, *very* difficult. The bureaucracy makes it so.

Ministers and political staffers are thrown into a department about which they may know very little. Bureaucrats, on the other hand, know the ins and outs of the departments and its files, and they have their own agenda regarding what ought to be passed into law. They play a game in which they try to outwit the partisan bosses and present false dichotomies and half-truths as options for policy reform. These two sides — the bureaucrats and the partisan aides — are constantly at odds. Most of the time one or both sides are leaking stories to the media, meaning the public gets a very distorted version of what is really going on. Unless the minister's office is filled with ambitious, clever and hard working staffers, it is the bureaucracy and not the minister that is driving public policy in Ottawa.

Have you ever seen an episode of *Yes, Minister*? It is shockingly similar to the experience in Canada's bureaucracy.

Third, the Prime Minister's Office. Staff in the PMO are the gatekeepers of change in Ottawa. Once a minister's office navigates the bureaucracy and determines tangible policy changes that could reduce the burden of government or change a law to give Canadians more freedom, it still must be approved by the PMO. As is well documented, the size of the PMO, particularly the number of staffers in communications, has skyrocketed. In 2011, there were a reported 1,500 government communications staffers in Ottawa, nearly 100 of them in the PMO. Their job is to study policy issues coming down the pike, and determine how reforms can be sold to the public. Looking through the lens of Public Choice Theory, political staffers are incredibly vulnerable. They are on the hook for any mistakes or bad publicity that result from reforms, so they are understandably risk averse towards any change. They would rather stick with the status quo, however Liberal it may be, than to make a change that risks bad press.

While political staffers are supposed to be there to help their ministers navigate a political agenda through the bureaucracy, in reality many have devolved into just another layer of Ottawa bureaucracy. This political bureaucracy is just as comfortable with the Liberal status quo of big government as the Liberals themselves.

Fourth, the opposition parties. In Canada, there are four opposition parties with elected members, and all exist on the left of the traditional political spectrum. They are all trying, to various degrees, to increase the size and scope of the federal government. The Liberal, NDP, Green and Bloc parties can all broadly be described as big-government parties. They all call for more: More regulations. More laws. More federal programs. More money. And these opposition parties drive much of the debate and policy discussions in Ottawa, through the media, Question Period, and committee. They have successfully managed to change the channel to discuss their priorities of more government.

Living inside the Ottawa bubble, advocates of limited government can feel like they are being attacked from all sides. That's because they are. A government town is a tough place to live for someone who wants to limit and reduce government. It makes sense, however, for parties on the left to revel in the Ottawa bubble.

Finally, *fifth*, the stakeholders, also known as special interest groups, who grace Parliament Hill daily to lobby for more: More spending. More goodies. More action. More intervention. These are self-interested professional lobbyists and organization whose job is to get something from Ottawa. I think of this as the tragedy of the commons for government resources. Everyone is fighting for a bigger slice of the pie for themselves and their special interest. There is no incentive for anyone to resist taxpayer handouts or leave resources for others, so it has become a free-for-all. And politicians of all stripes are beholden to these groups, often for political donations or coalition votes, and therefore do what they can to please these lobbyists.

This is the Ottawa bubble, and it is overwhelmingly in favour of more spending and a bigger, more powerful federal government. All the actors from these various groups have a predilection for government; that is what draws them in the first place. They believe in the federal government. And these influences easily disillusion free market activists. It is very difficult to maintain perseverance and principles when every day one is met with this overwhelming opposition. They question your worldview, your integrity, your patriotism and your morals. (I was called a "fascist" off the record by prominent reporters, on two separate occasions, for advocating limited government in a friendly, social environment.) Conservative politicians therefore, even those who hail from the West, are forced to govern under the norms of central Canada; the environment of big government. Regardless of popular opinion or common sense in most of Canada, politicians become entrenched in the poisonous environment of the Ottawa bubble. It compromises their ability to make decisions that run counter to the status quo. The Ottawa bubble peer pressure forces politicians to make even more bad decisions for the country, thanks to their yearning to fit in and be accepted in the capital.

This, in short, is why a Stephen Harper — who likely would have been president of a *Students of Liberty* or *Generation Screwed* student group on campus if they had existed while he studied at the University of Toronto and University of Calgary — could lead a government that introduced massive stimulus spending. Recall that over Christmas 2008, the Liberal, NDP and Bloc — Liberals, socialists, and separatists — staged an attempted coup d'état where they tried to merge and overthrow the newly elected minority Conservative government. They went to then-governor general Michaëlle Jean and asked her to reverse the election results and put this rag-tag coalition in power instead.

Why? One of the reasons they offered was the lack of economic activism over the recession. They demanded stimulus! These opposition parties wanted to undo the democratic decision of the 2008 federal election and replace the minority Conservative government because they wanted more economic activism in the face of the recession. What alternative did the Conservatives have, they argued, but to implement some kind of a stimulus package? At the time, I scoffed and mourned the death of fiscal conservatism in the Conservative Party. In retrospect, however, and after my experiences in Ottawa, I must say, I get it. Given the obstacles and opposition in Ottawa, it makes sense. Overwhelming forces skew the decision-making abilities of Conservatives in Ottawa; it makes them Liberal.

We can look, on the other hand, at the situation Jean Chrétien and Paul Martin encountered in 1994. They were battered by similar influences, but were pushed the other way. The vocal opposition

Reform party was demanding change. The media were out to embarrass the government after the Wall Street Journal reported on our debt and called our currency the "northern Peso." Stakeholder and citizen groups such as the CTF were demanding *less* from the feds, demanding they balance the budget. And even the bureaucracy was scared about the possibility of a default, which not only would be embarrassing, but would also mean a reduction in their benefits and perks. The Chrétien government's fiscal reforms were not led by ideology; they were forced by necessity. The Ottawa bubble told them they had to.

In order to win the battle of ideas, we must pierce the Ottawa bubble. We need libertarian and free market-minded people to assume positions and take action within these five various professions. Winning the war of ideas means shifting the focus of discourse, moving the goal posts of what is possible, and building a widespread consensus that liberty is better than dependency. We must convince the country that free market ideas are the most moral and the most efficient at truly creating wealth and lifting people out of poverty. Our philosophy helps the poor, folks in the middle *and* the well-off. Free markets are good for everyone. This certainly won't be easy. But as with the fiscal reforms of the 1990s, it can be done when given the right set of circumstances. The collapse of the welfare state and the failure of its programs will certainly provide such an opportunity.

FREEDOM CHAMPIONS

"The spirit of resistance to government is so valuable on certain occasions, that I wish it always to be kept alive. It will often be exercised when wrong, but better so than not to be exercised at all. I like a little rebellion now and then."

— Thomas Jefferson, letter to Abigail Adams, 1787

Because free markets are better than planned ones, and because liberty is better than dependency, the biggest challenge facing *generation screwed* is simply to communicate and convince others of these basics truths. Easy, right? This may seem trivial, but it is surely the greatest challenge facing all free market advocates around the world. Apathy and indifference can be equally as dangerous as malevolence and hatred. Low-information voters reign in Canada, and throughout the developed world. Many people engage in policy only during an election, when the campaign machines are in full gear and the truth is obscured by spin and politically expedient omissions. As short-lived Prime Minister Kim Campbell once famously said, campaigns are no time to talk about policy. But if not then, when? Most Canadians disengage after elections, letting politicians impose reckless or ruthless policies that destroy wealth, undermine basic freedoms, eliminate choice and further the trend toward dependency on the Nanny State.

I've spent a lot of time pondering how people develop an ideology, how they form their worldview, and why so many in Canada's intellectual elite side with big government. The same can surely be said in the US, the UK and most of the developed world. Whether it's wealthy actors, famous artists and musicians, mainstream journalists, celebrated public figures or even self-made business entrepreneurs, so many in the public eye tend to favour big government solutions. There are many theories to explain this phenomenon, but none better than that of the great Friedrich Hayek. In his essay, *The Intellectuals and Socialism,* he explains how intellectuals and academics have been co-opted by various brands of Marxist ideology; this worldview is then passed along through thought leaders and has a trickle-down effect throughout society. By looking at how this process occurs, we can learn a great deal about how to win the war of ideas, restore liberty as the primary good in society and beat the statists at their own game.

The Road to Serfdom

I earlier recounted the story of a young Friedrich Hayek — an economist and philosopher who exchanged letters with John Maynard Keynes in the 1920s — who was one of the greatest defenders of free markets and classical liberal philosophy in the 20th century. Hayek left his position at the University of Vienna, where he was influenced by Carl Menger and worked under Ludwig von Mises (both champions of the Austrian School) to begin teaching economics at the London School of Economics. Hayek refused to return to Nazi-occupied Austria and became a loyal British subject. In the years leading up to the Second World War, he began to notice some troubling similarities between fascism in Europe and creeping socialism in Britain. He challenged the academic elites' assertion at the time, that fascism stemmed from capitalism, and instead argued that fascism and socialism were the common ideology, as both believed in centrally planned economies and the concentration of power in a central government at the expense of individuals. Hayek was worried about creeping socialism and collectivism in Britain, and feared the wartime mentality to introduce collectivist policies that empower the state — at the expense of the individual. Liberty was being threatened by the power of the state, thanks to both socialism and fascism.

Hayek decided to do something about it. He wrote *The Road to Serfdom*, which was published in 1944 along with a condensed 20-page abridged version that was published in *Reader's Digest*. It is important to note that *Readers Digest* is not an academic journal, but instead an American general interest magazine that was read by millions. *The Road to Serfdom* was therefore able to both the ivory tower and the masses to reminded people not to abandon or forget the foundation of their society: economic freedom. Without economic freedom, Hayek argued, political and individual freedom would never have been achieved. Hayek instilled this lesson at a critical time in the US and the UK and helped ensure that the post-war economic order was based on free markets and economic freedom, not collectivism and central planning.

Public Intellectuals

The Road to Serfdom achieved both appeal and influence. It piqued the interest of Antony Fisher, a young war veteran who served in the British Royal Air Force. Fisher served alongside his younger brother, who was killed in the Battle of Britain. A sniper had also killed Fisher's father during the First World War, and these events made him an activist dedicated to defeating fascism and socialism in Britain and abroad. Fisher was a well-educated and successful businessman,

and was tremendously inspired by Hayek and the message of *'___*
Road to Serfdom. He was concerned that Britain had elected a Labour
government, and wanted to run for office to spread Hayek's warning
about creeping collectivism. He sought counsel from Hayek in
London, hoping perhaps that Hayek could be his economic advisor.
But Hayek instead talked Fisher out of a career in politics and told
him he could wield far more influence, and do far more good for
Britain and the cause of economic freedom, if he instead engaged in
the battle of ideas and public policy. Instead of running for office,

Fisher went to America and, upon the advice of Hayek, visited the
newly formed Foundation for Economic Education, where he
became convinced that think tanks were a better way to effect
political and social change. In 1955, Fisher started the Institute of
Economic Affairs (IEA) in London, which grew to become a leading
public policy think tank and paved the way for the Thatcher era
reforms in Great Britain. Building upon the success of IEA, Fisher
established the Atlas Economic Research Foundation in July 1981.
Atlas is a global network of free market think tanks, based in
Washington, DC, which supports and works with emerging think
tanks and freedom champions around the world. Through Atlas, and
with the strength and reputation of IEA, Fisher was able to help
create the Fraser Institute in Vancouver, the Centre for Independent
Studies in Sydney, Australia, the Manhattan Institute in New York,
the Pacific Research Institute in San Francisco, not to mention the
now 150 think tanks worldwide that Atlas has assisted and supported.

Hayek was right. Antony Fisher was able to influence millions of
people through public policy research and education; if he had
become a politician, he would have had to compromise his principles,
hold his nose as his party implemented necessarily populist policies
and risk being corrupted by power.

Dealers in Ideas

It would seem that Fisher influenced Hayek as well, as he went on to write an influential essay that touched on the advice he had given. In 1949, Hayek published *The Intellectuals and Socialism* in the University of Chicago Law Review, which also discussed the phenomenon of why universities and academics tend to favour socialism and big government solutions, and how these views creep into society at large. Many have the perspective that the academy does not matter, and that university professors and philosophers have very little influence on politics and "the real world." According to Hayek, this is incorrect. In the essay, Hayek explains how the ideas being sowed in university circles are passed throughout society by a group of people called intellectuals, whom he describes as "second-hand dealers in ideas." These are not philosophers or professors, but simply people who communicate ideas to the general public. Journalists, teachers, ministers, lecturers, TV and radio hosts, commentators, editors and writers (of both fiction and non-fiction), cartoonists, artists, even doctors, scientists, or anyone who calls themself an "expert."

Hayek's Second Hand Dealers in Ideas

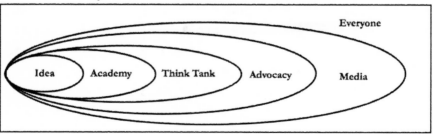

Ideas start with philosophers and then are discussed and taught by academics and university professors. These ideas are transformed into content and policy alternatives by think tanks and research centres. Advocacy groups popularize these ideas through publicity campaigns and the media. Journalists then report and editorialize to give the public information. All of these folks have a direct role in shaping minds and influencing policy. Popular culture and entertainment also play a role in public education and the dissemination of political ideas. Novels are often filled with social and political messages. Look at Ayn Rand and the success she has had in recruiting young people to an individualistic or libertarian worldview. From highbrow theatre to television sitcoms, there are thousands of encoded political messages that are communicated to, and subconsciously consumed by, audiences. They may not even notice the subtlety of Shakespeare's political dramas, or that Lisa Simpson is a political vegetarian, but these messages influence minds.

Or consider the influence that political satirists such as John Stewart, Stephen Colbert and Rick Mercer have on the political landscape, given that far more people tune into their shows than into any serious, policy-focused program. Socialism has managed to make so many inroads in society because there are so many left-wing intellectuals pouring out of universities and into these influential positions. These are the people who influence the world, drive the Ottawa Bubble, as discussed earlier, and determine the direction of our country. Unfortunately, the influencers who populate these occupations almost universally support the big-government status quo.

It is easy to see why this happens. From my experience, both in and out of university, the best free market minds are generally very logical, methodological thinkers, and therefore pursue careers in business, engineering and law. They become entrepreneurs and they build things. People who excel in an academic environment (dominated by socialists) tend to either stay in academia, or find careers that do not interact with the market, careers that are either sheltered or propped up by the government. They gravitate toward government bureaucracies or "government lite" institutions such as government-funded NGOs or the CBC. The more radical of this class goes to work for anti-capitalist advocacy groups and organizations (such as the organizers of Occupy Wall Street or those who run smear campaigns against Canada's oil sands).

Many of these educated elite also file into Corporate Canada or lobbying careers (often after doing a stint in politics), where they work to prop up the status quo and perpetuate the cushy relationship between big government and big business. Some may mistakenly believe that Corporate Canada is broadly a free market bunch. This assumption is wrong. Crony capitalism drives the business culture in Canada, and those working in government relations departments in big Canadian corporations are working to keep their special status and the deals they have negotiated with politicians.

While these activists may promote big government, there is an opportunity to lead our own movement for change in Canada. And it's pretty simple. Since intellectuals are the gatekeepers of ideas in society, we need to flood these positions with free market thinkers. Just like we need to puncture the Ottawa bubble, we need to build up a civil society that favours freedom through an army of freedom-loving public intellectuals. There are plenty of opportunities to be a second-hand dealer in idea, and every position can provide a tremendous opportunity to shape minds and achieve greater liberty. Whether you become a professor, a think tank researcher, a journalist or an activist; each serves a different, yet important piece in the puzzle. We need public intellectuals and intellectual entrepreneurs to fight this cause and spread our message. Even if you go it alone, it is easier than ever to start a blog or make a fundraising pitch online.
As Hayek notes, socialism is by no means a natural ideological fit for the working class or the poor, but instead something that has been imposed over time, through generations of successful intellectuals

and communicators. In order to communicate our ideas, we first need to convince people that our ideas are right. This may require that we are sometimes utopian, and perhaps even radical in our calls for a free market. We need to be bold, creative and imaginative.

LIBERTY OVER DEPENDENCY

"Socialism is a philosophy of failure, the creed of ignorance, and the gospel of envy, its inherent virtue is the equal sharing of misery."

— Winston Churchill

From both moral and economic perspectives, drawing on both philosophical reasoning and empirical data, no matter which way you cut it, free markets work. They have created more wealth and well being than any other model or set of policies. Allowing for economic opportunities so that individuals can lift themselves and their families out of poverty is a far better strategy than relying on government transfers and the welfare state. The former allows for transformation and lifts entire communities out of poverty. The latter merely creates a poverty trap and ensures dependency on others.

It is easy to champion freedom because we know that we are right. Capitalism and free markets have done more to help the poor and vulnerable than any other force in human history. China has a burgeoning middle class today, not because of the Communist Party and the planned economies that brought mass starvation and poverty under the dictatorship of Mao Zedong and his successors, but because of the great shift that opened up markets and brought capitalism and private property to the masses.

The Economic Freedom of the World Index — a Canadian invention that is now duplicated by research institutes and universities around the world — shows a clear and strong empirical link between economic freedom and higher levels of wealth, a better standard of living and even better environmental outcomes.

Most Free vs. Least Free Countries in the World in 2014

Rank	Most Free	Rank (/178)	Least Free
1st	Hong Kong	178th	North Korea
2nd	Singapore	177th	Cuba
3rd	Australia	176th	Zimbabwe
4th	Switzerland	175th	Venezuela
5th	New Zealand	174th	Eritrea
6th	Canada	173rd	Iran

The question is no longer even about the merits of a planned economy versus a free market; capitalism has long since won that battle. The data show that countries with greater levels of freedom have better economic, and therefore social, outcomes. These countries boast higher incomes, less corruption, longer life expectancy and greater overall happiness. Canadians now almost universally agree that markets create wealth, and this is done through individual creativity, risk and initiative. Governments do not create wealth. They can only take wealth and redistribute it.

If you believe there is a need for a "compassionate" government or a welfare state to help the poor and disadvantaged, ask yourself the following question: if you were a very poor member of the lowest social class, would you rather live in a free market economy like Singapore or Hong Kong, or a compassionate welfare-state society like France or Spain?

The free market powerhouses of Hong Kong and Singapore may not have elaborate welfare state programs, but they do boast endless economic opportunities to work hard, climb the economic ladder and achieve your own success. This is not an easy task, but it is possible and even commonplace. The welfare state societies of Europe, by contrast, will provide the poor and needy with endless social programs, but no jobs. Youth unemployment in Spain is approaching 60 per cent. If you are born poor in Europe, chances are very likely that you will remain poor throughout your entire life. In such free market economies as Singapore, Hong Kong and even Canada (we rank sixth in the world on this index), your economic status is fluid and there are opportunities for upward economic mobility.

Part of the major challenge for both freedom champions and for *generation screwed* is to convince people that government is not the solution. It is easy to ascribe an imaginary government solution, like "ending poverty" to help the poor or "banning handguns" to end violence, but in practice, these solutions never pan out. There are always unintended consequences, and many social ills in our society are simply not curable through legislation. You cannot legislate away basic elements of human nature, such as self-interest or self-preservation. And you sure cannot simply pass a law ban hatred or evil; if you could, we would have already.

If there were a panacea to ending poverty or murder, we would no longer be discussing these problems. But we are, and it is naive to think we can legislate the answers. As for the problems presented in this book for *generation screwed,* government cannot be the solution because government *is* the problem.

Let me say it again to be perfectly clear: government is the problem, not the solution. We have tried the big government way already: the idea that government policies can mend all of society's wounds and be all things to all people. We have experimented with big government in Canada since Lester B. Pearson and Pierre Elliot Trudeau. These big-government Liberals (who co-opted the word to its present-day meaning in Canada; in other parts of the world, they would be called Progressives, Social Democrats, Labour or Socialists) truly believed there wasn't a problem that couldn't be solved by adding another department to the federal government. They believed in big government and were willing to spend any amount necessary to impose big government solutions onto our country.

The Trudeau-era expenditures on "nation-building" programs became nothing but de facto slush funds for Liberal-friendly organizations and individuals. And all those new federal departments became a dumping ground for partisan Liberal appointees. Government spending sold to the public as the only way to keep Canada united, or a compassionate response to help the poor and the needy, in reality, simply built an army in Ottawa to defend the Liberal status quo of big government and the welfare state. And now we are going bankrupt because of this government activism.

We have tried their way, and it has failed us. Big government, activist government and the welfare state did not work. In Canada, this apparatus has not lifted the people out of poverty. It has not made our country a better, freer or fairer place. It merely gave false hope to millions, saddled millions more with unthinkable debt, and created a destabilizing dependency by many on the government.

And while our side has been stuck with the unfortunate title of "conservative" (we are not trying to conserve anything, we are radically trying to change the welfare state status quo), we are fortunate to be fighting for freedom. Folks on the left advocate for bigger government funded by the taxpayer and more heavy-handed intervention. They fight for government power at the expense of the individual; we fight for less government and more freedom.

We are ultimately charged with convincing people that liberty is better than dependency. Yes, free markets work better and produce more than planned economies. Yes, governments destroy wealth and make the economic pie smaller, thereby making us all poorer. Being free is better than being dependent. Government dependency should never be the goal. It is the least desired outcome. Our side wants to see people stand on their own two feet, to be self-sufficient and independent. This is true freedom. It is our job to convince people of this.

Overton Window

The ability of politicians to convince voters of a particular set of ideas, as demonstrated, is limited by their desire to win elections. Ultimately, politicians will do what they can to get re-elected, both individually, and as a party. It is not therefore the job of politicians to persuade Canadians of any one particular worldview or ideology. Politicians can only show that they are competent and trustworthy managers. Changing hearts and minds is the job of the intellectuals. Hayek's "second-hand dealers of ideas" are the ones tasked with convincing people of the merits of liberty and limited government.

Similarly, Joseph Overton of the Mackinac Center for Public Policy described the theory of the "window of possibility" in public policy. Now known as the *Overton Window*, the theory goes that at any given point in time, there is a range of ideas that are generally agreed upon and that the public will accept. It is a window of opportunity. And it is a very narrow window. A policy or political concept will only be viable if it fits within this window, regardless of what politicians may want or the country may need. Politicians themselves can only do so much to communicate and convince the public of their ideas, which must fit into the window in order to be accepted. It is the role of public intellectuals and idea leaders to expand this window.

According to the Overton Window, an idea begins as "radical." Many ideas in this book — much like many of the theories proposed by professors in university classrooms — are not broadly accepted by Canadians. It may seem very radical, for instance, to end the welfare state, given how reliant we are on it. But once the idea is proposed, people start to discuss it, and as people discuss it, many become convinced that it could work. It is no longer radical, but is still unthinkable to most. Ideas like shutting down the CPP or creating personal pension accounts are unthinkable at the moment. But eventually, enough people begin to champion this idea and propose an alternative to the CPP, like a personalized tax-free savings account or pre-funding of pooled retirement savings so your money is tied to you. These solutions are quite sensible, when thoroughly explained. And when the details and math are worked out, many will start to believe the idea is practical. If we can demonstrate how a young person will personally save hundreds of thousands of dollars over their lifetime, you can bet they will consider the reform practical. Heck, when you sell it this way — that replacing the CPP with a personalized pooled savings account means an individual's lifetime benefit will grow by half a million dollars — the policy would be extremely popular. And that, according to the Overton Window, is how to move a policy idea from 'radical' to 'popular,' and become policy.

Overton Window

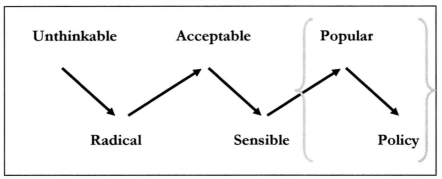

We should not blame the politicians for not having the stomach to ram free market ideas down the throats of Canadians. They are, after all, just doing their job and trying to get re-elected. If a free market politician were to impose a policy without first convincing the public of the merits of the reform, the people would not accept it, and eventually, both the policy and the politician would be rejected. People need to first be convinced that our free market ideas are the correct ones. And the responsibility for encouraging and educating people falls squarely on your shoulders and mine. It is our job to change the climate of ideas. *Generation screwed* has inherited a terrible mess and it is our job to clean it up. This can be done by changing the climate of ideas. We need to move the Overton window and convince people that liberty is better than dependency.

BETTER POLICY

"If you see ten troubles coming down the road, you can be sure that nine will run into the ditch before they reach you."

— Former US President Calvin Coolidge

"Life, faculties, production – in other words, individuality, liberty, property – this is man. And in spite of the cunning of artful political leaders, these three gifts from God precede all human legislation, and are superior to it. Life, liberty, and property do not exist because men have made laws. On the contrary, it was the fact that life, liberty, and property existed beforehand that caused men to make laws in the first place."

— Frédéric Bastiat, *The Law*, 1850

This book has offered a guide for *generation screwed* to take back its future. While there is plenty wrong with our political and social structures that have led to creating *generation screwed*, a future of poverty is not a foregone conclusion. I am optimistic that things can and will turn around. Many of the suggestions and ideas for turning the tides are long-term and strategic; they may take decades, if not generations, to make progress. These solutions, however effective and important, are somewhat unsatisfying for young, idealistic utopians fighting for change. Luckily, there are many things we can do and call for today that will quickly help ease the burden of big government. We need better policy, and this chapter offers a few of the most promising free market policy solutions that can shift dependency away from big government, and empower individuals to take back control of their lives.

As with any social, political or economic problem, there are no silver bullets. Complicated and difficult problems are solved by complicated and difficult solutions. And, as suggested in these opening quotes, government and policy are often *not* the solution, and may often make the problem worse. As supporters of limited government, we need to be ever aware of the limits of using legislation and regulations to solve big problems. With that in mind, these policy proposals are a step in the right direction and would help to reverse the many trends that are working against *generation screwed.*

The Problem: Big promises made by politicians during election campaigns can be very costly. Often the ideas sold to taxpayers do not include a price tag. When politicians take office, they believe they have a mandate to implement their campaign promises, despite the fact that they only presented one side of the coin (the benefit) while hiding the other (the cost).

Policy Solution: Make them prove it. Require all politicians to cost out their campaign promises, and tie spending to proven revenue sources. If politicians promise to introduce new universal day care, they should be required to explain how much this promise will cost taxpayers, and how that money will be raised. This is a measuring stick that we can use to actually hold politicians accountable. It also gives voters more information and knowledge about the choice they make. If a government promises full-day kindergarten at a price tag of $2 billion per year, paid for by increasing sales taxes by one point, then at least voters can make an informed economic decision. By demanding all promises be costed out and tied to a revenue source, voters would receive a more full picture of what is actually being presented. No more "free" goodies. The public would also be given an added tool of transparency. If the government promised a $2-billion price tag for a program, and the cost inflates to $2.5 or $3 billion, the public can easily see the inefficiency and broken promise.

The empowered public needs to start treating their government — funded with their money — the way shareholders treat publicly traded companies. Every dollar should be easily traced, transparent and accounted for. If we had real transparent and open government, every dollar spent would be made proactively accessible to the public. Revenues should be transparently tied to spending projects. For instance, all revenues collected from gasoline and diesel taxes should always go towards transportation infrastructure funding. We should be able to track how every dollar is spent, the timeline for projects from start to finish, and the bidding process for tendering contracts (including the winning bid and the terms of the contract). The more information we have about our government (and its often shady wheeling and dealing) the better. This is what transparent government ought to look like. Technology is making this possible, and we should demand that every dollar spent by our government be available online to be scrutinized by the public. It is increasingly self-evident that this is how governments should operate. Being opposed to greater transparency is inherently against democracy.

The Problem: There are too many government bureaucrats, often underworked and overstaffed, with lucrative salaries and benefits, plus taxpayer-funded pensions that require constant bailouts and carry multi-billion-dollar unfunded liabilities.

Policy Solution: Let them retire, and don't hire replacements. In some cases, Manitoba for instance, as much as 40 per cent of the government sector workforce will retire within the next decade. We should just let them go, and retire the position alongside the worker. There is so much redundancy and title inflation within the civil service that we could certainly stand to shed a portion of it without anyone noticing. We hear a lot of talk about "wage freezes" on government salaries, but a more important freeze would be a hiring freeze. Young people should be discouraged from joining the government, and a hiring freeze would send that message.

The Problem: Our public insurance and pension plans (CPP, OAS, GIS and Ontario's proposed Ontario Retirement Pension Plan) are incredibly unfair to young workers, who have to contribute more money than ever and can expect lower and lower returns when they retire. They are unsustainable in the long run, and there is no guarantee you will get anything in return for the $7,000 per year the typical worker forks over in CPP and EI taxes.

Policy Solution: Take the money back. Shut down these failed and out-dated Ponzi scheme-style government pension funds and build a new retirement savings system that focuses on the individual, with personal or personalized pooled savings accounts.

In 1981, Chile replaced its national defined-benefit pension plan (much like the CPP) with a new defined-contribution system. All new workers were required to join this defined-contribution plan. Existing workers had a choice, but most chose the new system in which they could decide where to invest their retirement savings. The results were surprisingly positive in many ways. The new fund has created a 50 to 100 per cent increase in retirement benefits for workers, and according to an OECD report, has created a more equitable system that has promoted economic development, improved labour market conditions for workers and given the overall economy a big boost. It is no coincidence that Chile has recently passed Argentina as the richest country in Latin America. Market reforms such as personalized pensions have led the way.

Australia's reforms have been equally successful. Also set up in the 1980s in the face of an aging population and insufficient funding in state pensions, Australians are now required to contribute nine per cent of their income into an individual account, which gets pooled into a national investment fund. Upon retirement, each Australian gets a lump-sum payout based on their contributions, employer contributions and the market performance. Typically this means over a million dollars paid out, providing individual Australians far more freedom and flexibility to the recipient. The individual retirement plan extends to 92 per cent of Australians who own a share in this savings pool, and is valued at over 100 per cent of Australia's GDP.

In the long run, the benefits of personal pension accounts far outweigh the short-term pain of making the switch. In both Australia and Chile the decision has paid dividends. Allowing individuals to be in the driver's seat of their own retirement savings has helped create a financial strategy with long-term sustainability that is fair to all workers. These kinds of programs work to promote retirement freedom, as opposed to dependency on government.

The Problem: Politicians spend on whatever projects they can dream up, and don't face any real limits on what they can imagine and impose. Hence every government in Canada has overspent through much of the past few decades, resulting in annual deficits, spiralling debt and interest payments that will be dumped on the shoulders of young and future taxpayers.

Policy Solution: Give politicians an allowance. Limit what they can do and what they can spend. Governments must be controlled, and we need to stop mission creep and jurisdiction creep. For instance, why does the federal government have a department of health? Health care is a provincial matter, clearly falling under provincial jurisdiction according to the Canadian constitution. The feds should butt out. Similarly, retirement savings has long been a federal issue; Ontario should be prohibited from stepping in and building another retirement pension program on top of the CPP. It is out of line with Canadian tradition and precedence, and should not be permitted.

As well as limiting mission creep, we need to curb government's spending abilities. A perfect example of this kind of limit is already in place for many governments in this country, as most Canadian municipalities are not permitted to borrow for program spending. They cannot run operating deficits. They can borrow and amortize the cost of infrastructure programs, but they cannot borrow to pay salaries or build more social programs. This is a good start, and we should work to extend this to all Canadian governments.

The Swiss go even further, in legislating a spending cap (known as a "debt brake") that prohibits politicians from increasing spending faster than revenue growth. It holds the government's growth rate to that of inflation plus population growth. This debt brake was introduced in 2003, and the result is that government spending has dropped from 36 per cent of GDP to 34 per cent, during a decade when all of Europe and North America moved the other direction. The Swiss spending cap enforces responsible government. It also follows Dr. Daniel Mitchell's *Golden Rule:* that the economy should always grow faster than the government.

The Problem: Politicians and governments operate within short election cycles and even shorter news cycles. This leads to a heavy tendency towards short-term and often short-sighted decision making, at the expense of future taxpayers.

Policy Solution: Introduce an intergenerational watchdog. Irresponsible politicians need to be held accountable and reminded of the long-term consequences of their bad ideas. Hungary has found a solution for this problem, by creating a new position in government called the Hungarian Parliamentary Commissioner for Future Generations. The job is like that of an ombudsman, and the individual is given a significant amount of independence to represent the public — in this case the future public — by investigating and addressing complaints, studying issues, and making recommendations on laws and policy.

Now, I am very sceptical and usually opposed to creating new government offices and empowering bureaucrats. But the ombudsman position can be a rare exception — if it can prevent the waste and misuse of taxpayer dollars, and shine a light on government waste and corruption. An ombudsman for future generations could be tasked with ensuring that programs such as pensions, Medicare and employment insurance are equitable, and that reforms will be fair for younger people and future taxpayers. This person could also voice concerns about deficit spending, borrowing, the high costs of interest and leaving debt for future generations. The role can go further than monitoring intergenerational fairness on the tax front. In Hungary, the role has become colloquially known as the "green ombudsman" — since he works to ensure that resource development policies are not short-sighted, aims to prevent ecological degradation, promotes curbing pollution and encourages policies to keeping the environment clean.

The Problem: Widespread apathy, undeserved trust in government and a romantic view of politics has led to the exponential growth in government at the expense of our individual liberties.

Policy Solution: Admittedly, this is less of a policy solution and more of an advocacy solution. Two American organizations, Open Data and Project Veritas, work to expose the truth about the nature of government and its ugly side. These are two examples pulled from hundreds of advocacy organizations that exist in countries like the US, but that have no Canadian equivalent, thereby creating an excellent opportunity for young Canadian activists to create similar initiatives in Canada.

Open Data is a citizens' group that collects government data and connects it with individuals to shine a light on local spending. You can go online or onto the app, enter your zip code or location, and Open Data will provide heaps of information about government spending in your area. It shows the numbers of government workers, salaries, government contracts and projects using taxpayer money in your city or town. The organization uses freedom of information and access to information laws to collect mountains of data about government at all levels. It then uses geo-mapping technology and a smart app to make local information easily accessible. Government accountability requires transparency. This not only exposes bloated government, but also helps disseminate information broadly and engage the grassroots.

Project Veritas has a similar mission — to expose government waste and engage the public — but goes about it in a totally different way. It uses hidden video, disguises and clever Gotcha!-style journalism to expose the truth about some US organizations that receive taxpayer funds. Project Veritas has successfully exposed hate-driven and morally egregious behaviour by quasi-government organizations. By exposing the truth — be it corruption, misuse of funds, bigotry within government, backdoor deals, *quid pro quo* arrangements and so on — Project Veritas helps people see the ugly side of government. This group has also successfully engaged young people and folks who may not care much about policy or economics.

Both of these organizations are examples of how exposing the truth in creative ways and utilizing new technology can help *generation screwed.* Our society's reliance on government is dangerous; discrediting the government and showing what it truly is — a bunch of rent-seekers and self-interested busybodies — can dissuade people from that unhealthy and unsustainable dependency.

FINAL REMARKS

"Freedom is never more than one generation away from extinction. We didn't pass it on to our children in the bloodstream. The only way they can inherit the freedom we have known is if we fight for it, protect it, defend it and then hand it to them with the well-thought lessons of how they in their lifetime must do the same. And if you and I don't do this, then you and I may well spend our sunset years telling our children and our children's children what it once was like in America when men were free."

— Former US President Ronald Reagan, March 30, 1961

We will win. Our ideas are better. We just need to work harder. Understanding the problem is half the battle. Once we know where the problem lies, we can focus our resources and attention on addressing and fixing it. As more citizens become aware of and knowledgeable about intergenerational unfairness and the burden of big government, we can work together for the united goal of saving our country's future and your lifetime economic prospects.

We are engaged in an ongoing battle of ideas, and in many ways, we are still fighting and refighting the battles of yesterday. The anti-development and anti-capitalist groups simply rehash the stale and failed doctrine of Karl Marx, while the big-government lobbyists and debt apologists regurgitate the failed polices of John Maynard Keynes. Luckily for us, we get to champion the ideas of such brilliant minds as John Locke, Adam Smith, Friedrich Hayek and Milton Friedman. We should use the lessons of these classical liberals to guide our thinking on markets and economics, and remind us of the importance of individual liberty in maintaining and building a free society.

Just as the fall of the Berlin Wall was inevitable, so too will be the fall of the welfare state. Communism is counter to human nature. In the USSR, chronically low productivity across all sectors of the economy — an inevitability with no monetary incentive for hard work or greater output — meant that by the late 1980s the Russian economy could no longer feed itself. It no longer produced enough food, and could not afford to import enough food to feed its people, let alone its satellite states in Eastern Europe. Economics and the free market played their course.

In retrospect, the broad consensus of historians now posits that the collapse of the Soviet Union was inevitable, given the inherent weaknesses in the USSR economy caused by central planning. Communism was morally wrong; it was economics, however, that dealt the fatal blow.

Economics will similarly deliver the fatal blow to the welfare state, a system that lives beyond its means, tries to be all things to all people and sacrifices the future on behalf of the present. But we need not wait for the walls to come tumbling down. *Generation screwed* is well-equipped to champion a new concept of the role of government in our society.

But it will take action on your part, and on the part of *generation screwed*. So, go out and talk to your friends. Help spread this message. Convince your peers and classmates to read this book, and join the movement. If you are a student, check it see if there is already a liberty-oriented student group on campus. There likely is. If not, create one. And if you need any help, you know where to find me.

Make sure you check out my website — www.candicemalcolm.com — for more resources, stories and updates about *generation screwed*.

You have all the tools you need, and you will solve this problem.

Yours in liberty,

Candice

READING LIST FOR LIBERTY

Aside from all the books they give you to read in school (and I highly recommend reading all the great works, both those with which you agree and disagree), for a more thorough understanding of the classical liberal and free market worldview, as promised, here is your "summer reading list" for liberty.

There is a reason we are classical liberals. It is thanks to the original "liberals" — Locke, Mill, Hume, Kant, de Tocqueville, Smith, Jefferson, Bacon and Aquinas, who were inspired by the ancient Greek philosophers: Plato, Socrates and Aristotle. Reading these thinkers will help to establish a framework of the enlightenment and the advent of liberalism. This is a great place to start, and if you are so inclined, I encourage you to become familiar with the works that have built the foundation of the free market and classical liberal worldview. It is important to know where we came from, what we believe (whether or not you personally believe it) and the strengths and weaknesses of our arguments. You do not need a degree in economics or political science to master these topics. You can be a freedom champion and second-hand dealer in ideas by simply reading and understanding some or all of these great works.

Friedrich Hayek:
Road to Serfdom, The Fatal Conceit, Constitution of Liberty

Hayek Essays:
Use of Knowledge in Society, The Intellectuals and Socialism

Frédéric Bastiat:
The Law

Bastiat Essays:
Bootleggers and Baptists, The Candlemakers' Petition

Henry Hazlitt:
Economics in One Lesson

Milton Friedman:
Free to Choose, Capitalism and Freedom

Thomas Sowell:
A Conflict of Visions

Ludwig von Mises:
Human Action

Leonard E. Read:
I, Pencil

George Orwell:
1984, Animal Farm

Orwell Essay:
Politics and the English Language

Robert Nozick:
Anarchy, State and Utopia

Ayn Rand:
The Fountainhead, Atlas Shrugged

Barry Goldwater:
Conscience of a Conservative

Brian Doherty:
Radicals for Capitalism

PJ O'Rourke:
Eat the Rich

Amity Shlaes
The Forgotten Man: A New History of the Great Depression

ACKNOWLEDGMENTS

I'd like to start by thanking Troy Lanigan and the entire CTF organization, past and present, for their dedication and commitment to a free society in Canada. It's easy to imagine how much worse things would be for *Generation Screwed* if we didn't have such a fierce government watchdog. A special thank you to Generation Screwed campus coordinator Aaron Gunn for giving me the first opportunity to speak to students and deliver this message. In compiling that Generation Screwed presentation, I realized the severe importance of this message, and was moved to write this book. Thank you to the Generation Screwed students for challenging me and championing this message every day. This book is written for you, and I look forward to the creative solutions you will bring forth to fix the problems laid out on these pages.

A big thank you to my editor Bruce Annan for his thorough insights, and to my brother, Fraser, for his thoughtful suggestions. You both made this book much better.

This book is about debt, and I am indebted to my many mentors, friends and colleagues who have challenged my views and been great catalysts of my career. Since this is my first crack at writing a book, I'd like to include a thank you to those who have provided support, friendship and guidance: Brittany Malcolm, Drew Malcolm, Fraser

Malcolm, Amber Malcolm, Rachel Worthen, Erynne Schuster, Patricia Schuster, Tricia Foster, Kristy Todd, Jackie Korol, Jessa-Lynn Meidinger, Riki Hanna, Sara Ilnitsky, Vanessa Schneider, Tim Mak, Vita Ramos Trevino, Kristen Cone, Rodrigo Felix Montalvo, Stefania Hronn Gudrunardottir, Maria Cañadas, Theresa Gallagher Dahl, Lowry Wyman, Lavina Lee, Peter Gillies, Lulu Yang, Michael Whitfield, Chad Wilcox, Isaac Morehouse, Trevor Burris, Maria Anderson, Rachel Venezia, Arielle Roth, Joseph Humire, Alejandro Chafuen, Kristina Krane, Vitor Marciano, Krista Nelson-Marciano, William MacBeath, Brock Harrison, Danielle Smith, Howard Anglin, Jason Kenney, Ana Curic, Hamish & Kathryn Marshall, Matt Wolf, Dennis Mathews, Chad Rogers, Mike Wilson, Charles Adler, Brett Tarver, Rikki Ratliff, Althia Raj, Scott Hennig, Mark Milke, Gregory Thomas, Nick Bergamini, Stephen Taylor, Matt Bufton, Adrianne Batra, Lorrie Goldstein, Anthony Furey, Jerry Agar and Michael Binnon.

Easily the biggest support has come from my family; I'm blessed to have parents that have given abounding support and provided tremendous opportunities throughout my life, not least of which providing me with many books to read and much time to read them. I also managed to marry quite well, and inherited another set of loving, caring and protective parents in Toronto. *Mamnoon, kheili doosetoon daaram*, Maryam, Amir and Kia.

Finally, thank you to my incredible and brilliant husband, Kasra, for his love, encouragement, insight and wise council. Every girl should be so lucky.

ABOUT CANDICE MALCOLM

Born and raised in Vancouver, British Columbia, Candice has moved across the country and around the world studying philosophy and economics, while advocating for liberty, free markets and limited government.

Candice completed a Koch fellowship in Washington, DC, and has worked at the Fraser Institute, the Atlas Economic Research Foundation, as a special assistant to Danielle Smith and the Wildrose Party in Alberta, and as press secretary to Minister Jason Kenney in Ottawa. She is currently the Ontario Director of the Canadian Taxpayers Federation, a weekly columnist for the Toronto Sun and a blogger for the Huffington Post.

Prior to her appointment with the CTF, Candice was the Director of Research at Sun News Network. She has a Bachelor of Arts in Political Science from the University of Alberta, a Master's in International Relations and a Master's in International Trade and Commerce Law from Macquarie University in Sydney, Australia.

When she isn't advocating for lower taxes and less government, Candice is usually spending time with her large family (she has five siblings and three awesome nephews), watching hockey (or playing – she once scored a triple hat trick in minor hockey), or off travelling somewhere. She's been to every continent, loves exploring new places and was once a travel writer. She now lives in Toronto, and spends significant time in San Francisco with her husband, Kasra.

CPSIA information can be obtained at www.ICGtesting.com
Printed in the USA
LVOW06s2039020415

433053LV00001B/66/P